Accolades

"Rani St. Pucchi's designs are absolutely beautiful!"

—**Alison Krauss,** SINGER-SONGWRITER

"Rani, thank you for designing such a beautiful gown. I can't tell you how privileged I feel to wear one of your creations. You are so talented. My St. Pucchi wedding dress was a work of art!"

—**Candice Crawford,** WIFE OF DALLAS COWBOYS QUARTERBACK, TONY ROMO

"I've gone to countless awards and worn countless dresses, but nothing compares to Rani's designs. I got the inspiration for my entire event from my St. Pucchi dress. I felt elegant and beautiful and special. I felt like a queen.

—**Sanya Richards-Ross,** OLYMPIC GOLD MEDALIST

"Rani St. Pucchi is the most incredible wedding designer in the world, in my opinion. There are no other dresses like hers; they're so beautiful and so elegant and fantasy and pure beauty. When you put it on you feel like such a girl and you feel beautiful; very fairytale."

—**Tara Reid,** ACTRESS

"Words cannot describe you as a person or a designer, Rani, you are so incredible. The love and time you spent in making my St. Pucchi dress perfect is something I will never forget. You are responsible for making me feel truly like a bride and I can't thank you enough!"

—**Debbie Dunning,** ACTRESS

"I always admire people who take the time to share with the world what they have as their gift. Rani St. Pucchi is such a person- a unique blend: a fashion entrepreneur, an experienced and gifted designer, an innovator, a pioneer. She is exactly what the world needs: we need wisdom, we need people who, like Rani, open up their experience and let people learn by sharing it. She is an inspiration, a champion all the way. Rani has a deep understanding of how powerful it is to be elegant and classic and proves that dressing your best as you walk down the aisle to say "I Do" lends power and shows security in self."

—**Edward Tyll,** RADIO PERSONALITY AND HOST OF THE SYNDICATED RADIO SHOW THE ED TYLL SHOW.

"In *Your Bridal Style* Rani wonderfully illustrates step-by-step on how to prepare for that most important day as brides walk down the aisle to say "I do". As the foremost designer and pioneer who introduced color to the US bridal scene, Rani shares her knowledge and experience of more than 30 years with brides all over the world. The concepts shared in *Your Bridal Style* will help brides plan their wedding with ease and create a positive and powerful self-confidence as they journey thru the myriad steps on designing the wedding of their dreams"

—**Walt Shepard,** FOUNDER AND PUBLISHER, INSIDE WEDDINGS

"Written by a true expert, *Your Bridal Style* goes beyond the trends to help brides define their own individual style. Brides everywhere are looking for advice and guidance on how to plan their wedding with ease. Bridal fashion is personal and intimate. In *Your Bridal Style* Rani gives you the inspiration to be free of convention—to express your personal view and the way in which you wish to come across on your most important day. *Your Bridal Style* is a comfortable fit for every bride."

—**Jim Duhe,** VP/ASSOCIATE PUBLISHER, BRIDAL GUIDE MAGAZINE

"Rani made my wedding day magical and memorable. From the moment I walked into her St. Pucchi salon I knew there would not be another designer but Rani for me. The dress she designed for me was the most exquisite, elegant yet somehow sexy. Rani's demeanor, grace, patience, and elegance made our experience that much more meaningful and special. *Your Bridal Style* is more than just a book about dressing to flatter your body. It is a tool every bride needs as she is planning the wedding of her dreams. Thank you, Rani, for making me truly feel like a princess bride. I am forever grateful.

 —**Angelle Grace Wacker**, SENIOR VICE PRESIDENT, NAI CAPITAL, INC.

"Rani is an amazing designer who truly is in love with fashion. She creates designs that are ageless and become a calling card for all the lucky brides in her world. Her designs speak these powerful words . . . super chic, flirtatious, imaginative. Collections that have a beautiful presence, that speak for your body and give women a glow of confidence, an elegant vision, and a radiant sense of being happy. How a bride dresses and presents herself is the picture she paints for all to see. Rani's personal spirit, style & uniqueness is why she has chosen to share with us such intelligent words and give guidance and strength to brides on their most important day. Looking and feeling fabulous empowers women to be fabulous! Rani is one of those powerful fabulous women."

 —**Barbara Tilzer-Frankel,** CREATIVE DIRECTOR

"Rani has raised the standard of 'couture' in the bridal industry with her luxurious, highly-coveted gowns of exquisite silk and embroidered detail ~ she is truly one of industry's finest in couture bridal styling".

 —**Margaret Rowe,** MARGARET ROWE COUTURE JEWELRY

"I cannot stress enough how exquisite, unique, and timeless Rani's gowns are. St. Pucchi gowns are truly in a league of their own. I still pinch myself thinking about how amazingly blessed I am to have had the opportunity to work with Rani and to have a St. Pucchi gown. We shared visions and ideas, and then began trying on dresses. Rani is as kind as she is beautiful, and her creative mind is awe-inspiring.

My St. Pucchi wedding gown is one of my most cherished possessions that I will surely keep all the days of my life. My groom, Calen, said that the very first moment he saw me walking down the aisle to meet him, I literally took his breath away. I don't think there are enough words to express my overwhelming adoration for St. Pucchi. The St. Pucchi experience is like that of a fairytale. I cannot thank you enough Rani for all you have done".

—**Elizabeth Garner**, St. Pucchi bride

" I felt like the most beautiful woman in the world on my wedding day, and it was all because of Rani and her amazing dresses at St. Pucchi. She is a true artist, a true professional, very warm and personable, a designer who truly cares about her brides. I could tell that she really cared about making my special day truly special. I feel truly blessed and honored to have met Rani and to have worn her gorgeous designs".

—**Mary Futcher**, St. Pucchi bride

"I've always been hypnotized by the intricate and elaborate details of a St. Pucchi garment. It's a work of art and very non-traditional in today's standards, which is why I chose to wear one of her unique pieces on my very special day. I felt like I was transported through time in a funnel of tulle, crystals, and lace!!
I LOVE my dress!"

—**Athena Portillo**, St. Pucchi bride

"Once I tried my St. Pucchi dress on, it was magic.... my feet went gliding through the store & my heart sang. Only one other thing in my life had ever felt like this, and that is my Christopher. I knew in that moment, this was the perfect gown for me in every way. I want to give credit and heartfelt thanks to the creative & talented mind of designer Rani aka "St. Pucchi" who not only made this gown, but also created a one of a kind matching veil for me to wear that complimented me & the gown perfectly! It was the most breathtaking wedding gown I could've possibly had. I will treasure & preserve it along with the wonderful memories it holds. Thank you for helping make our Wedding Day the most memorable day ever. I felt like an angel & it was a truly magical day. I couldn't have done it without you!!! Thank you so very much, Rani, for your talents & for creating my absolute dream gown & veil. It was perfect!"

—**Tara Zampella,** St. Pucchi bride

"There truly are no words to describe how I felt about my St. Pucchi wedding gown, I guess the closest word would be 'magical'. From the lace sleeves, to the intricate blue beads along the edge of the lace, everything was magical".

—**Catherine Gendel,** St. Pucchi bride

"I am in love with my dress from St. Pucchi! The attention to detail is just amazing. I personally feel that this is the type of dress that gets handed down generation to generation. Thank you St. Pucchi for helping us make our wedding day a special day!"

—**Tania Binning-Rotondi,** St. Pucchi bride

"*Your Bridal Style* is a wonderful book for those who have some knowledge of the bridal world as well as those who are just beginning to find their way into planning the wedding of their dreams. If you have any questions about finding your way to class, style and a timeless way of designing your overall bridal look, this book is your answer. Lovely, simple way of learning the tricks of how to dress that flatters every body type, to planning each step along the way to the most important day of your life, to the moment you say, "I do". Rani is a first-class designer, a wedding expert, a true treasure".

—**Chanda Montroy,** De Luz, Temecula, CA.

" I was so inspired by a particular St. Pucchi design that no matter how many wedding dresses I tried on, none measured up! I knew St. Pucchi would be my designer, whose dress I wanted my future husband to see me in. My dream dress came to life, and even as I write this tears fill my eyes looking back on how lucky I was to find my St. Pucchi dress, the one that was my inspiration for my wedding in Waikiki, Hawaii, and that will live in my memory forever. Thank you Rani for designing my dream dress!"

—**Brigitte Patton**, St. Pucchi Bride

"The Gowns and dresses designed by Rani and her design house St. Pucchi are nothing short of Epic . . . Completely timeless from another time. Walking down the aisle in a dress designed by Rani is transformational. No one is designing gowns like hers anymore… Rani's vision speaks to you the moment you lay eyes on one of her creations. Extraordinary. Being in a room surrounded by St. Pucchi creations is nothing short of one huge 'Aha' moment."

—**Deborah Newman**, La Mesita Ranch Estate

Your Bridal Style:
*Everything You Need to Know to Design
the Wedding of Your Dreams*

by Rani St. Pucchi

© Copyright 2017 Rani St. Pucchi

ISBN 978-0-9976977-7-3

All rights reserved. No part of this publication may be reproduced, stored in a retrieval system, or transmitted in any form or by any means—electronic, mechanical, photocopy, recording, or any other—except for brief quotations in printed reviews, without the prior written permission of the author.

Book interior designed by Rani St. Pucchi

Gowns by St. Pucchi

Published by

St. Pucchi

P.O. Box 27254
Los Angeles, CA 90027
www.stpucchi.com

erything you need to know to design the wedding of your dreams

YOUR
BRIDAL
STYLE

Rani ST. PUCCHI

You were born together, and together you shall be forevermore.
You shall be together when the white wings of death scatter your days.
Ay, you shall be together even in the silent memory of God.
But let there be spaces in your togetherness.
And let the winds of the heavens dance between you.

*L*ove one another, but make not a bond of love:
Let it rather be a moving sea between the shores of your souls.
Fill each other's cup but drink not from one cup.
Give one another of your bread but eat not from the same loaf
Sing and dance together and be joyous, but let each one of you
be alone,
Even as the strings of a lute are alone though they quiver with
the same music.

*G*ive your hearts, but not into each other's keeping.
For only the hand of Life can contain your hearts.
And stand together yet not too near together:
For the pillars of the temple stand apart,
And the oak tree and the cypress grow not in each other's shadow.

—KAHLIL GIBRAN, "ON MARRIAGE"

Contents

DEDICATION...III
INTRODUCTION....................................... IV

CHAPTER 1: Congratulations, You're Engaged! 10

CHAPTER 2: Your Wedding Planning Timeline 16

CHAPTER 3: Your Wedding, Your Way:
              Your Venue, Your Destination, Your Style . . . 36

CHAPTER 4: Your Wedding Budget 58

CHAPTER 5: Lines That Flatter:
              Choosing a Style for Your Figure. 70

CHAPTER 6: Wedding Dress Silhouettes 85

CHAPTER 7: Fabrics, Laces, and Trims 116

CHAPTER 8: Commonly Used Terms Every Bride Should
              Know Before Dress Shopping 134

CHAPTER 9: Shop Talk: *From Window Shopping to
              Your Walk Down the Aisle*. 140

CHAPTER 10: The Budget-Savvy Bride:
               Online, Sale, or Rent? 158

CHAPTER 11: Color in Your Wedding. 166

CHAPTER 12: Is Nude the New White? 178

CHAPTER 13: The Crowning Glory: *The Veil*. 184

CHAPTER 14: **Finishing Touches:**
Embellishments and Accessories 190

CHAPTER 15: **All About the Bustle** 198

CHAPTER 16: **What Goes Underneath:**
Your Intimate Apparel. 203

CHAPTER 17: **The Photo Shoot.** 210

CHAPTER 18: **The Wedding Planner** 218

CHAPTER 19: **Bridesmaids:** *Yes or No?* 225

CHAPTER 20: **Mother of the Bride** 230

CHAPTER 21: **Getting in Shape for Your Wedding Day** . 236

CHAPTER 22: **Wedding Day Mishaps** 242

CHAPTER 23: **Marriage Legalities.** 246

CHAPTER 24: **After the Wedding** 252

CHAPTER 25: **FAQ: 53 of Your Most Pressing**
Questions Answered. 258

CHAPTER 26: **101 Wedding Tips** 298

THE EVOLUTION OF BRIDAL FASHION
AND FINAL THOUGHTS 310

ABOUT THE AUTHOR. 322

ALSO BY RANI ST. PUCCHI 325

This book is dedicated to all those who encouraged me to fly toward my dreams. My life would have been entirely and regrettably different if I didn't love fashion and all things beautiful.

To all my clients and my brides—those who have shown loving support of my work—you continue to inspire me. And to all those embarking on this exciting journey of planning the wedding of their dreams, know that planning a wedding is beautiful, but planning a marriage is priceless. I would love nothing more than to see you walk down the aisle on the arm of your beloved—happy, joyous, and fulfilled.

Take your time. Do it right. Enjoy.

Introduction

There's something so powerful about going back in time and reliving the key moments of your life. Memories about events you had not thought about in a long time: what you have been through and where you have come from—a history of your successes, if you will.

And it begins with a dream . . .

For me, it all started with the hit television soap opera *Dallas*.

Friday nights were my favorite. I was hooked on the show, and in such awe of the glamorous clothes and the big hair the women wore, their lifestyle, the tall glass buildings—just about everything that *Dallas* stood for, and I visualized moving there one day.

I was living in Bangkok, Thailand, at the time running a tailoring business at a prestigious hotel. Although I had no design experience, I became quite proficient in designing women's ready-to-wear just because of my intense love of fashion and all things beautiful.

Dallas was my inspiration. I studied the extravagant fashion shown on the screen and would sketch for hours. It helped that I grew up around fine fabrics and laces, my family being the largest purveyors of fine lace in Thailand. Aside from my love of books, I had always lived and breathed fashion.

Among the affluent clientele I catered to in my tailoring salon was a beautiful lady from San Antonio, who visited me often. I would help her with her wardrobe and design her extravagant evening wear and suits. During one of her visits in 1984, she asked if I would support her charity event with my designs.

I couldn't believe it. Wasn't San Antonio close to Dallas?

I was excited beyond words, and before I knew it, I was on a flight to San Antonio with my fifty-two-piece ready-to-wear collection.

As I was preparing the collection and planning the order in which each outfit would appear, I thought it would be wonderful to have a wedding dress as the finale of the show. So, I whipped up a blush-colored Thai silk, hand-embroidered dress, and hand-beaded it with Swarovski crystals.

Little did I know that the one dress that I had designed as an afterthought would forever change my life. The show was a huge success, but more importantly, the roar that sounded when the finale dress came out on the runway was deafening!

The Universe works in mysterious ways. As luck would have it, the leasing agent of the Dallas Apparel Mart happened to be in the audience and invited me to bring my bridal collection to showcase at the Mart's Bridal Fashion Week that was happening in six months.

Wait! Should I not mention that my bridal collection consisted of just this ONE dress?

The ONLY bridal dress I had ever designed in my life . . .

But of course, *she* didn't need to know that. And I wasn't about to tell her!

For someone who had no design background and was clueless about wedding dresses, it was a daunting thought.

My heart was beating so fast . . .

Dallas! This was a dream come true.

I hesitated, wondering if I had the talent, and more importantly, the money and the resources to honor such a huge commitment. But that thought only lasted a split second as I found myself saying, "Yes, of course! I would be honored."

As someone who had spent years dreaming about one day living in Dallas, I was totally convinced that the opportunity given me was nothing less than a divine intervention. I had a fire in my heart and a calling on my life that I trusted would play out.

I had more questions than answers right then. When I had the dream of one day living in Dallas, I had no clue as to what career I would follow, nor how I would be led there. All I knew was that perhaps, if I stopped mulling and stressing over the "how" and just followed that small tug on my heart, then it would lead me right where I needed to be.

And so here I was. Saying "yes" to my dream.

This was a time of celebration.

I had been fortunate enough to manifest the first step. Now came the hard part. It was time to be real. Time to set a clear goal of what, exactly, this *life* in Dallas was going to be about.

How was I going to not only make a living, but also be a success at my craft?

Having accepted the offer to show my "bridal collection" at the Dallas Apparel Mart, I prayed that the Universe would back me up.

There was no time to waste. I had only six months to put together my collection. My goal was very clear: to be a success and to make my mark in an industry that I was pretty clueless about, in the city of my dreams, and in a country that I knew without a doubt I would adopt as my "home" one day.

I wrote down a detailed list of everything I would need: the funds required, the types of fabrics and laces, jewels and notions, and the biggest challenge of all at the time—to come up with creative and unique ideas for my first bridal collection.

"*Your dreams are only your dreams until you write them down . . . then they become goals.*"

I set myself small steps on my way to completing the bigger goal so that I would not feel so overwhelmed.

And I *visualized*.

I visualized every dress.

I designed it first in my mind.

I saw the embroidery details.

I started sketching feverishly, and ideas started pouring out.

I worked with fabrics and notions, colors and patterns.

Designing bridal gowns was a spiritual experience for me. Although the designs flowed through me, I knew it was really the Divine doing the work. It was as if I was in a trance.

I visualized the success of my first bridal show, and in my mind's eye I saw the press and buyers loving each creation. I saw orders pouring in.

The collection now ready, I flew from Bangkok to Dallas, Texas.

On April 15, 1985, the day before my first bridal show, I registered my company, "St. Pucchi," on a wing and a prayer.

I decorated my showroom at the Dallas Apparel Mart with much anticipation and excitement. I had no clue what other designers would be showing, since every showroom window was shrouded with opaque sheets of paper so that no one could peer in.

This was my very first show, and I designed and decorated the showroom the best way I knew how, mostly based on what I had seen on the TV screen, especially on the series *Dallas.*

Sixteen mannequins on raised platforms of differing heights, clad in my handiwork, decorated the six-hundred-square-foot showroom, with one form behind each glass window on either side of the entrance.

This was the collection I was called to design, the one that I prayed would launch me as a bridal designer in America.

The day the show opened, I looked at the displays in all the other showrooms around me, and my heart skipped a beat.

Oh my God! What had I done?

All around me was a sea of white—white in every window, in every showroom, on every floor of the building.

And my sixteen-piece St. Pucchi bridal collection was entirely in color.

Blush, butterscotch, and even pale blue . . .

I had not designed a single white dress.

I felt I had really messed up!

I had not taken the time to study the US bridal market and had not known what the accepted norms were in the American bridal world.

How could I know?

Growing up in Thailand, I saw only colored wedding dresses, mainly blush-colored ones. Weddings were a celebration—in color. White was mostly worn during mourning.

Buyers would walk past my showroom, stop, and gasp. The press would swarm around and flashes would go off as they eagerly photographed away.

People were flabbergasted by such a controversial concept, and I could hear their thoughts loud and clear: Who was this designer? How could she even think that America would embrace color in bridal wear?

It didn't matter what others said. What mattered was that *I* believed in what I was doing. I felt passionate about my work and felt so deeply in my heart that I had finally found my calling.

This audience didn't really understand me yet.

Or perhaps the audience I was seeking didn't live at this address...

Designing was my passion, and fashion my calling. I knew that now. I felt as if I was the witness hovering above and watching as things unfolded.

Curious and breathless...

At the end of the second day of Bridal Fashion Week, I had not taken a single order. I was starting to get seriously concerned.

I kept looking at the showrooms around me and at the buying frenzy that was going on. Every showroom was filled to the brim with people writing orders and shaking hands and laughing.

And here I was, across the hall from them, with no action except for the press taking frantic notes and photographers snapping pictures with their cameras.

I looked wistfully at my beautiful babies—my creations, the luxurious colorful wedding dresses all waiting to be touched and admired.

This was the most beautiful collection I had ever designed in my life.

There was something about the idea of fantasy and fairy tale that connected a narrative to my designs, something escapist. It was historical, unabashedly feminine, and lavish in its use of color and fabrics—all pure silks—at a time when none of these were in fashion and never before used in bridal wear.

And I knew it was only a matter of time before buyers would take notice.

They say ignorance is bliss.

Lo and behold, the next morning, as I walked into the glass building and made my way to my showroom, a stack of *The Dallas Apparel News* piled up on the front desk at the foot of the elevators stopped me in my tracks.

My heart skipped a beat as I looked at my face staring back at me from the front page of the bridal industry's most revered paper.

The headline read: "ST. PUCCHI DESIGNS DREAM-LIKE GOWNS!"

The media wrote about my courage and daring in upsetting the industry norm and hailed me as the pioneer for introducing color and silk fabrics to the US bridal scene.

The American bridal industry as we knew it had changed forever.

I could not believe my eyes and was so encouraged and humbled by the recognition. I wanted to shout from the rooftops! But I kept my composure and headed to my showroom.

There was a line of buyers waiting for me to open the doors.

And I wrote orders.

The rest, as they say, is history . . .

Within eighteen months of setting my goal and visualizing, I was nominated as the Best Bridal Designer in Dallas.

At the same time, I designed evening wear and special occasion dresses. Buyers and the press welcomed the novelty of and the unique concepts in my designs.

I continued to receive nominations in this and many other categories, finally receiving the highest honor in the US.

My first DEBI (Distinctive Excellence in the Bridal Industry) award as the Best Bridal Designer was received in October of 1990, just a few months shy of my five-year goal.

Since then, my designs have been recognized globally and I have since received numerous other awards.

Today, St. Pucchi dresses have been shown on every major catwalk across the world, featured in every major magazine and media outlet, and appeared on numerous TV shows, most notably on the hit TV sitcom *Friends*.

I have personally worked with more than fifteen thousand brides and women of distinction and have dressed numerous celebrities, artists, singer-songwriters, and sports personalities.

All this would have never been realized had I not followed my dream, visualized, and taken massive action!

But that was not the end of my journey. There was so much more for me to learn and many more mountains to climb.

There was still work to be done.

The book you are holding in your hand was at one time but a thought, a dream, a visualization, a belief.

You see? Success, just as life, is a journey, not a destination.

Now I want to ask you: What is YOUR dream?

You are reading this because you are embarking on a life journey, one you have decided to share with your significant other.

You have a vision of a life you wish for yourself, with the love of your life. And I am here to help you with some of your decisions to get you off to the right start. For the rest of this book, I will be your best friend and hold your hand through the ins and outs of planning for your big day.

I have personally worked with more than fifteen thousand brides since I launched St. Pucchi, and I know the challenges you face.

If there is one piece of wisdom I would share with you, it is this: Be unique in doing what you want and not what others expect. Stay true to yourself and draw from your and your partner's mutual likes and dislikes, get to know and accept your shared personal history, food tastes, childhood memories, and family traditions, and have a wedding that reflects your shared values.

Many couples share a beautiful life but lose sight of their love as soon as they begin designing their wedding. They become slaves to others' expectations, to what the media says they should do, and throw their common sense out the window.

The most difficult decision is behind you. You have met and chosen "The One." Meeting your soul mate is the most precious step in this journey called marriage.

Now, to planning your wedding . . .

Shall we begin?

Chapter One

CONGRATULATIONS, YOU'RE ENGAGED!

One question, one simple answer, and your life has forever changed.

You said "Yes" to the man of your dreams. *Congratulations!*

Laughing, crying, grinning till your cheeks are sore, you've become that wonderful cliché: The Happiest Woman in the World.

If you were involved in deciding which type of ring you received, then you know the process was somewhat agonizing, yes? After all, a diamond is very personal and very precious. Besides, it's the longest style commitment you will ever make.

So, what does your diamond say about you?

Did you know that each one of the seven most common diamond cuts reflects your personality?

Oval: One of the most popular diamond shapes and great for the bride who loves an elegant yet classic aesthetic.

Round: For the woman who wants a traditional look that will be timeless and classic and maximum sparkle, this is the diamond for you.

Marquise: For the bride who knows her mind and moves to the beat of her own drum, who wishes to create the illusion of elegant, long hands, this pear-shaped diamond is perfect.

Emerald: For the discerning bride who wishes to exude elegance and refinement, somewhat understated yet classic with an edge, the elongated shape and step-cut faceting of this diamond is perfect.

Asscher: Graphic and timeless. For the woman who loves the retro look and old-world sophistication, this is the diamond for you.

Cushion: Feminine and trendy, perfect for the bride who wants a soft and gentle look with lots of sparkle. The curved corners and brilliant facets of this diamond provide all that and more.

Radiant: If you have a bubbly and outgoing personality, love lots of sparkle and flash, then the brilliant faceting and rectangular shape of this diamond is the one for you.

Luckily, diamonds never go out of style, so whichever sparkler you chose, it is the prefect one for you.

How excited you must be as you start thinking of your upcoming wedding! So much to do, so many decisions to make . . .

Perhaps you are a little confused, somewhat overwhelmed.

Fret not. I can help you get there. But first things first . . .

You will want to share the wonderful news with your most important family members and friends before the rest of the world finds out. People can be sensitive, especially if they find out secondhand about your big decision. This way, you're showing them how much you care.

The days when everyone else discovered your big news via the announcement section in the Sunday edition of the local paper are behind us. Social media is most definitely the new platform. So, go ahead and share ring selfies and hashtags to communicate your new relationship status. Make sure to include your significant other when sharing your joy.

Next, you may want to plan an engagement party. This is not mandatory—many couples today don't have one at all. If you do, then plan on having it soon after you get engaged—ideally, within three months. Hopefully, by then, you have set a wedding date, as this is the first question everyone will certainly pose to you. An engagement party is a great way to gather together to celebrate and is especially nice to have if your families don't know each other well so they can get better acquainted.

Think of the engagement party as a kickoff to all the wedding events that will happen on your way to the altar. It can be as simple as having a cocktail party at your or someone's home or as extravagant as renting a club or your favorite restaurant. The party is often hosted by one or both sets of parents, or if an aunt or a close friend wants to host the party, that's fine too. Just don't expect someone to host one for you. Engagement parties aren't an obligation.

Usually only family and close friends are invited to the engagement party, so don't feel like you have to invite a ton of people. It's totally fine to keep it intimate. Just make sure not to invite anyone who won't be on the wedding guest list.

You may want to have a small registry ready since guests might want to give you an engagement present. Remember, though, that people are not obligated to bring gifts, so don't be upset if guests arrive empty-handed.

What you'll wear depends on the formality of the event and the venue. If you are going formal, then an evening gown would be appropriate and help you stand out. Shorter dresses with interesting details, perhaps with lace trimmings, are a good choice for a casual outdoor affair.

Once the initial excitement has settled down, you'll want to lay some groundwork for your wedding. If you're like most women, while you may have envisioned the man you will eventually marry, you probably don't have the vaguest idea of how to go about planning a wedding and where to start.

In the next chapters, I will guide you through the morass of details involved in planning a wedding, from picking a wedding date to planning and divvying up your budget to sidestepping sticky social situations.

Read On...

CHAPTER TWO

YOUR WEDDING PLANNING TIMELINE

No secret here: Planning a wedding is intense.

There are so many crucial things to be done and decisions to be made. Worse still, if you happen to be a perfectionist, the stress level alone can soar off the charts! You soon realize how long your to-do list is, from shopping for your wedding dress and accessories to setting up the guest list, planning the wedding theme, and finding the venue.

Very soon, you may find your own ideas slipping through the cracks as your well-meaning friends and relatives step in to "help" with their advice and recommendations. Isn't it amazing how everyone wants to weigh in? Too many voices can cloud your vision. Eventually, it can take all the fun out of your wedding.

Take heart. You can manage it all. Yes, you can!

There are hundreds of truths you know about yourself, so start by writing down everything that you love, everything that gives you joy. Close your eyes, and what do you see? What are your favorite colors, hues that you love? Your favorite foods?

Flowers? How about your favorite venue? Do you see a castle with crystal chandeliers and red roses? Do you see yourself in nature and dancing under the stars with your sweetheart? Perhaps at the beach? Listen to what your heart is saying, trust it, and know that it will not steer you wrong.

As the process unfolds and you have all your ideas, plans, and inspirations on paper, you will find that you feel calm, collected, and confident. Now you know what you want and can start researching venues and vendors and planning your timelines. Now you can split the tasks—those you will personally handle and those you will delegate—and assign dates to each one of them during the various stages of wedding planning. Now you are better equipped to see the process through with great success and pride.

Have fun as you go on this journey so that you are not scattered and stressed out. With all that you will be doing, make sure to pause and take care of yourself. Wedding planning is important, yes, but what is more important is to occasionally stop whatever you're doing, smile, dance, laugh, and spend quality time with your fiancé. Never allow the process to make you lose sight of the reason you're doing this, nor the strength and depth of your love for each other. After all, you are creating memories. Make them good ones!

Due to the many differences between weddings, you may find some of the reminders listed in this chapter don't really apply to you. Or, perhaps a few particular details that are part of your special plans are excluded from this list. Modify the checklist as you go along until you're satisfied it's tailored to your needs.

Your checklist at a glance:

NINE TO EIGHTEEN MONTHS AHEAD

___***Announce your engagement:*** Your first responsibility as a newly engaged couple is to inform your families and close friends of your decision to marry. Traditionally, the bride's and the groom's

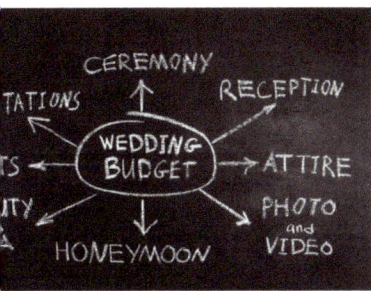

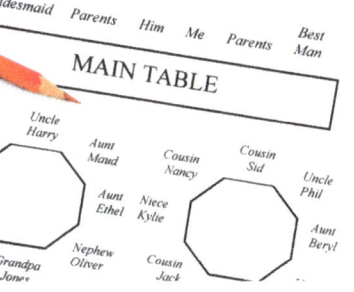

parents are informed first. If the families have not met before, a get-together should be arranged. An engagement party may be appropriate at this point.

___**Pick your wedding date:** Once the engagement is official, it's time to decide tentatively, in consultation with both families if possible, on the date most suitable for all parties. Weigh your ideal date against any inconvenience to your family and your guests. As much as possible, avoid a month or season when people will have trouble getting away from work or other obligations.

___**Meet with your officiant:** Consult your officiant before choosing a firm date and time for the ceremony. There may be restrictions on the date (no weddings during Lent, or no Jewish ceremonies on a Saturday, for instance) or the time of day. If you do not belong to a religious congregation but do want to be married in a place of worship, you may have to shop around, as many places are not available for weddings of couples who are not regular members of their congregation. Meet with your officiant to discuss the ceremony.

___**Decide on the budget and who's paying for what:** If the two of you are paying for the wedding, you may want to pick a date that allows you enough time to save. If your families are sharing the expenses, then modern etiquette holds that any division of expenses is mutually agreed upon; no one should be commanded to cover particular expenses. Once you've reasonably tallied your wedding funds, you'll have to divvy up the dollars to include the wedding, reception, clothes, honeymoon, and other miscellaneous expenses.

___*Hire a wedding planner (if you want one):* If the planning process is overwhelming, consider hiring a wedding planner who can help you plan and budget for the entire event or merely certain aspects of it. Meet with a few, check their references and testimonials from their previous clients, and obtain bids.

___*Compile a guest list and organize addresses:* With your fiancé, agree on how large or small the wedding should be, and a rough estimate of the number of guests you would like to invite. Choosing whom to invite can be a tricky issue. To prevent hurt feelings later, clarify the extent of his and your families' involvement in the guest list early on. Let common sense and circumstance be your guide. You could make it a four-way split, with your parents, his parents, and the two of you each inviting one-fourth of the guests. Write up the guest list.

___*Choose a wedding theme and style:* Most weddings fall into four basic themes:
- *Traditional*—A grand hotel ballroom, a country club, or a banquet hall.
- *Destination*—A beach, an island, or the mountains.
- *Casual, outdoor*—Your or your parents' backyard or a county park.
- *Trendy*—A restaurant, a downtown loft, or the atrium of a contemporary art museum.

Based upon your desired theme and style, research and determine the décor for your reception.

___***Create wedding inspiration boards:*** This helps you compile information, collect your thoughts, and add inspiring ideas and pictures to sort through and organize as well as share with your family and friends. Inspiration boards can include the following: wedding theme, color palette, wedding dress, accessories (such as veils, shoes, and jewelry), wedding stationery, cake, venue, reception décor, hair and makeup, table settings and centerpieces, bouquet and floral arrangements, party favors, bridesmaids' dresses, groomsmen's attire, etc. This can be a corkboard on a wall, a folder, or an online inspiration board.

___***Book the ceremony site and reception venue:*** As soon as the wedding date is set, research venues for the reception. If an outdoor wedding is planned, the tent supplier will need to be booked at this time. If the ceremony and reception will be held in a park or recreational area, obtain necessary permits. For very popular reception venues, reservations should be made more than a year in advance. Choose ceremony and reception venues, negotiate contracts, and leave a deposit. Schedule a rehearsal date and time. Secure parking and/or transportation for your guests at the reception location.

___***Book the wedding photographer and videographer:*** Set up appointments, review portfolios, set your budget, etc. so you can make a decision. The best photographers and videographers are booked six months to a year in advance, so you may want to get the ones you want booked early on. Make a list of photos you would like, such as ceremony and reception shots, and make sure to go over these in detail with them.

___***Reserve the musicians/DJ:*** If you want to hire a musician or musicians other than those associated with your place of worship, contact them now, but not before consulting with your officiant regarding rules that outside musicians may have to comply with. Ditto for the DJ/live music at the reception—ask the catering manager for rules and restrictions that may apply. Music is the key to the tone of your reception, so take your time and involve your fiancé to the max. Decide on the mood you want to inspire and take your time to pick the music—R&B? Salsa? Rock?—to make it happen. Make sure it fits the theme of your wedding. Book the band or DJ.

___*Hire a caterer:* Meet with several caterers and arrange for tastings so you can narrow down your choices. Perhaps your reception location offers on-site food service or is affiliated with a catering service. Either way, decide on your budget, style of service, and the menu. Make your selections and book.

___*Research and interview florists:* Compile a list of flower arrangements required for the wedding and consult a florist regarding design, composition, and color. If possible, choose flowers that are in seasonal bloom to contain costs. If your wedding will be taking place during a religious observance, check with your ceremony officiant about any restrictions regarding the kinds of arrangements that can be used. Floral arrangements might already be displayed in celebration of a religious holiday!

___*Hire a stationer if you're going custom:* Long before guests glimpse your gown, admire the flowers, or taste the main course, they receive the invitation. So, it's crucial to make this first statement about your wedding an effective one. Your invitation expresses both who you are as a couple and the essence of your wedding. Identify your style, and think about the mood you're trying to create. Modern? Romantic? Casual? This must be conveyed throughout all your stationery: save-the-date cards, invitation and response cards, programs, seating cards, place cards, menus, and thank-you notes. Decide what feeling you want to convey and either go with standard available options or hire a designer and place your order.

___*Determine your honeymoon location and budget:* Your honeymoon location depends on several factors, such as your budget, personality, preferences, time available, and season of the year. So, determine your budget, plan how much time you can take off, decide on the type of place you would like to visit, and consider weather conditions at the destination at the time of your visit. If you find it difficult to decide, create individual dream lists and compare them so that you can make an ideal choice that is mutually satisfying. Check out potential destinations online and visit travel websites or consult a travel agent for ideas and suggestions. Plan and book early to find the best offers.

___**Select the bridal party:** Choose potential members of your wedding party and ask them to participate in your celebration. If you have a lot of close friends but a small guest list, consider limiting the bridal party to one or two attendants only. Save the key supporting role—maid or matron of honor—to the relative or friend who means the most to you and is the person likeliest to come through for you.

___**Look through bridal magazines and online for attire ideas:** Now that you have gone through the above steps and have a clear idea of the type of wedding you are having, it's time to gather ideas about what you would like to wear. To narrow down the most flattering silhouettes for your figure, read my book *Your Body, Your Style: Simple Tips on Dressing to Flatter Your Body Type*, or read Chapter 5: Lines That Flatter: *Choosing a Style for Your Figure*. Pin styles you are drawn to on your online inspiration board or save them in your scrapbook. Plan your wedding look and begin your dress search.

___**Visit local bridal stores to browse through their selection of gowns:** Deciding how you will look at your lifetime event is perhaps the most exciting part of all your planning. Begin to shop for your bridal gown and headpiece. Your wedding dress choice will be influenced by the type of wedding you want—formal or informal, big or small, cold or warm weather. Try on dresses in silhouettes that flatter your figure. In rare cases, a bridal designer will customize a particular style to suit your needs. Because wedding gowns can take as long as ten months to deliver, go ahead and select and order your gown and accessories, including veil and shoes.

___***Register for gifts:*** Choose your tableware and linen patterns. List your gift selections with the bridal registry at your favorite store or website. Make sure you have the high-end basics covered when putting together your wedding registry—and don't forget the fun stuff here and there, too!

___***Pick out your wedding cake:*** Cakes are an essential factor of any wedding. Depending on your theme and budget, you can either go ultra-traditional and pick a classic tiered cake or add a new-age touch by going the route of cupcakes. Now, the real question that you and your partner have to ask is, What flavor do we want? Flavor options in the cake world are endless. You can go with a classic chocolate cake with chocolate buttercream icing or lemon poppy seed with a raspberry filling or a white sponge cake with rosewater-infused frosting. Some cake designers can even design your cake to match certain elements of your wedding dress. The options are limitless. Research cake designers and arrange for cake tastings so you can determine exactly what works best for you.

___***Send save-the-date cards:*** Make sure guests mark their calendars and get excited about your wedding. You can either get cards printed or put a twist on tradition with save-the-date magnets as wedding reminders your guests can put on display.

___***Order bridesmaids' dresses:*** By now you know the color and theme of your wedding. Choose and order bridesmaids' dresses and accessories.

FIVE TO NINE MONTHS AHEAD

___***Review details with consultant:*** If you have hired a wedding planner, review and finalize your wedding details with them.

___***Finalize guest list:*** Discuss and finalize the guest list with both families. Compile the names of all out-of-town guests and work out any social activities you'd like to plan for them.

___***Book a block of hotel rooms for out-of-town guests:*** Research airline, hotel, and rental car options for guests. Consult a travel agent or visit travel websites. Negotiate rates and make advance reservations to lock in at the best rate.

___***Plan your honeymoon details:*** Plan your days and activities during your honeymoon. If you are going abroad on your honeymoon, ensure that you both have valid passports and apply for any visas or necessary immunizations.

___***Decide on your speakers:*** Make a list of who you would like to have speak at your reception and in what order. Confirm with your chosen speakers and go over details with them.

___***Plan your ceremony:*** In consultation with your officiant, plan the details of your ceremony. When making your appointment, ask when you can meet with the organist, if desired.

___***Groom's, groomsmen's, and ushers' attire:*** Discuss attire with your fiancé and the groomsmen, and request that they go to local formalwear stores to try on tuxedos. Though most formalwear rental outlets can often supply garments quite quickly, ideally the groom should narrow down what to wear and make rental arrangements for himself and the groomsmen and ushers at this time. The best man could help with this process, and arrange for a final fitting a week before the wedding to allow for last-minute alterations.

___**Select attire for the flower girl and/or ring bearer:** If you have decided to include little ones in your party, you may want to select their attire now.

___**Shop for wedding bands:** Research a variety of wedding ring styles. Narrow them down to the styles you like most and go to jewelers to try them on. If you plan to have wedding rings custom-made, you may need more time. Ask your jeweler well in advance. Select and order your wedding rings.

___**Decide on food and liquor:** Make your final decision on the food and liquor to be served at your reception. Finalize the menu of what you would like to serve your guests. If your catering manager is not handling the liquor needs for the wedding reception, contact a wine and liquor representative at this time. Make arrangements for a liquor license, if required.

___**Finalize musical selections:** Prepare a playlist of musical selections for your reception and go over the details with your band/DJ.

___**Sign up for dance lessons:** Choose a song that means something to you, something that reminds you of special moments together, maybe something you listened to a lot when you met. This way, your dance will always be romantic. Find a good teacher and practice, practice, practice. The more you do, the less nervous you will be on the day.

___**Purchase bridal accessories:** Shop for shoes, stockings, jewelry, and lingerie, and make sure the overall look and feel fits your vision of how you wish to present yourself on your big day.

___**Go to your first gown fitting:** Bring your shoes, stockings, jewelry, and lingerie with you when you go for your first gown fitting. Your first fitting is where you make sure everything is exactly as you imagined.

___*Notify bridesmaids about dress fittings:* Confirm an appointment for your bridesmaids to have their dresses fitted.

___*Place print orders:* Determine the design, wording, font, and paper stock of your wedding stationary and finalize your order. Arrange for a printer or hire a calligrapher for table cards. Make sure you have enough time to review and approve your order.

___*Order confetti:* Choose and order something fun, such as rose petals or confetti, for guests to throw after your ceremony.

TWO TO FOUR MONTHS AHEAD

___*Apply for a marriage license:* Start making the necessary plans to acquire your marriage license.

___*Order your wedding cake:* This is a good time to place your order.

___*Plan your rehearsal dinner:* Make reservations for the rehearsal dinner and select your menu.

___*Plan your bachelorette party:* Discuss bachelorette party plans with your attendants.

___*Plan your bridesmaids' get-together:* Plan a luncheon or dinner for your bridesmaids.

___*Try on your wedding attire:* Try on your full wedding attire at this time to make sure there are no last-minute changes or alterations needed.

___*Confirm delivery of the bridesmaids' dresses:* If the bridesmaids' dresses are color-coordinated, make sure they are delivered per your order. Have the bridesmaids try them on and go through fittings.

___***Secure wedding day transportation for guests:*** If you're providing transportation to the ceremony and reception for your wedding party, then make sure all arrangements are finalized.

___***Review and approve wedding announcements and printed program proofs:*** You will need a couple of weeks to address and mail all the invitations and six weeks for them to be received and responded to by your guests. If there are many out-of-town guests, you may want to send them out sooner.

___***Finalize choice of honeymoon destination and make reservations:*** Make sure all plans are confirmed and details checked off.

___***Honeymoon wardrobe:*** Purchase honeymoon clothing, luggage, and accessories.

___***Book a room for the wedding night:*** Ask for a wedding suite at your hotel and let them know that it is for your wedding night. Hotels usually offer special incentives.

___***Finalize details for post-wedding brunch:*** Secure the venue and select a menu for the post-wedding brunch.

___***Discuss the prenuptial agreement:*** If you plan to have a prenuptial agreement, meet with your attorney to discuss it. Have all legal papers drawn up and ready to be signed by both parties.

ONE TO TWO MONTHS AHEAD

___***Mail the invitations***: Invitations should be mailed six weeks prior to the wedding date.

___***Create hotel information cards:*** Include maps and hotel information cards with your invitations.

___*Plan the rehearsal:* Plan the ceremony rehearsal and the rehearsal dinner, if applicable, at this time.

___*Send rehearsal dinner invitations:* Make sure everyone invited receives them.

___*Purchase wedding favors and attendants' gifts:* Shop for wedding favors. Select and purchase gifts for the wedding party.

___*Purchase a gift for your fiancé:* Shop for something that will have sentimental value and be a keepsake for years to come.

___*Buy guest book:* This is for guests to sign and is a convenient reminder of to whom to send thank-you cards.

___*Have legal and other requirements in place:*
- Obtain marriage license and request certified copies.
- If you intend to change your name, prepare the necessary documents.
- If your state requires blood tests, make appointments.
- Send change-of-address information to the post office.
- Contact local newspapers about publishing wedding announcements.

___*Have your hair and makeup trial:* Make an appointment with stylist to discuss your wedding hairstyle and makeup.

___*Finalize details with the photographer and videographer:* Make a checklist of what you expect and go over all the final details to avoid any miscommunication, misunderstandings, and stress.

___*Confirm floral order:* Finalize floral arrangements with the florist and arrange for delivery of flowers and other decorations on the big day.

___***Arrange for the getaway car:*** Finalize arrangements for transportation to the ceremony, reception, and your wedding night destination.

___***Finalize all deliveries:***
- Confirm delivery and pick-up times for all attendants' attire.
- Make delivery arrangements for your wedding cake.

___***Choose your wedding vows:*** Or, if you plan to personalize your vows, write them now.

___***Finalize the details of your ceremony with your officiant.***

___***Meet with the ushers and assign them duties.***

___***Secure a dressing room for your bridesmaids for your wedding day.***

___***Finalize your honeymoon plans*** and confirm all reservations.

___***Arrange for transportation*** to and from the airport (if flying) or car to your honeymoon destination.

___***Write thank-you notes:*** It is best to do this as you receive or open your gifts.

ONE TO TWO WEEKS AHEAD

___***Have your final dress fitting.***

___***Arrange for pickup of the bridal ensemble.***

___***Update the registry.***

___***Research gown preservation companies:*** Make arrangements to have your gown treated after the wedding day.

___*Coordinate final fittings for the groom, groomsmen, and ushers:* Schedule final fittings and the pickup of the rental garments for the groom, groomsmen, and ushers. Arrange for the return of the groom's tuxedo within a day or two after the wedding.

___*Go in for a dry run with a professional makeup artist and schedule your day-of-the-wedding appointment.*

___*Schedule a manicure/pedicure for the day before your wedding.*

___*Pick up your marriage license.*

___*Finalize and memorize your wedding vows.*

___*Write toasts for the rehearsal dinner and wedding reception.*

___*Finalize arrangements with your catering manager and liquor representative, if needed.*

___*Submit a final shot list to your photographer and discuss positioning with your videographer.*

___*Send your final playlist to your DJ or band.*

___*Arrange for preparation, storage, and break areas for the musicians/DJ at the reception venue.*

___*Review RSVPs and contact guests who have yet to reply to your invitation.*

___*Finalize the list of reception guests.*

___*Confirm the final headcount with your caterer and review details, preferably in writing.*

___*Finalize the seating chart.*

___*Arrange for table cards to be set up at the reception venue.*

___Determine the placement of programs at the ceremony venue.

___Give last-minute requests to the vendors.

___*Prepare the fee or donation for the officiant and tips for the vendors in labeled envelopes:* Ask the maid or matron of honor or best man to distribute them.

___Confirm your honeymoon travel arrangements.

___Start packing for your honeymoon.

___*Pick up your wedding dress* (if you haven't already).

___*Break in the wedding shoes at home:* Make very sure they are comfortable.

___Prepare announcements to be mailed immediately after the wedding.

___Designate someone to look after your home while you are on your honeymoon.

___*Find out where guests will be staying:* You may plan to deliver welcome notes or gifts to their rooms.

THE DAY BEFORE

___Finish packing for the wedding night and the honeymoon.

___Reconfirm transportation arrangements for the ceremony and reception.

___Do last-minute primping: This may include nails and self-tanning.

___Rehearse the ceremony and attend the rehearsal dinner.

___*Give gifts to the bridal party: If you choose, give gifts to your and your fiancé's parents to thank them for their support.*

ON THE DAY

___*Give wedding rings to the best man and maid or matron of honor to hold.*

___*See hairdresser and makeup artist:* Beautify.

___*Remember important items:* Don't forget the car keys, wedding rings, marriage license (if not already given to the officiant), keys to your home, airline tickets, passports, money, and honeymoon hotel accommodations.

___*Load your luggage:* If you are driving your car to your wedding night destination, have the car driven to the reception site with your luggage in tow.

___***Give yourself plenty of time to get ready:**** Be dressed and ready for the photographer or videographer about two hours before the ceremony, or as agreed.

___***Bride should transfer her engagement ring to her right hand.***

Relax and enjoy yourself!

The only regret many brides have when the wedding is over is: "The day passed by so quickly!" Make the most of every minute by pausing every now and then to take in and enjoy the scene. Be hospitable and appreciate your guests, but at the same time, don't let any guest monopolize your time for too long, since there will be many other people to meet and greet. Everyone remembers a good host, and just a few minutes with each guest is all it takes to convey the message that you appreciate their presence.

Seize Every Moment!

This is your day!

Chapter Three

YOUR WEDDING, YOUR WAY:
Your Venue, Your Destination, Your Style

Fashion has become more of a personal statement.
Gone are the days when brides were forced to conform to strict rules about what they could wear depending on when and where the ceremony took place. Bridal fashion had a direction. For instance, the fashion police used to ban trains for informal evening and daytime weddings, while enforcing that veils be as long as the trains for very formal evening ceremonies!

But no more! What was considered appropriate, or not, for different types of weddings, seasons, venues, has become increasingly blurred.

Do you feel great in a sheath? Wear a sheath!
Do you want to forego wearing a veil? Certainly, go ahead!
Does the weather still matter? No.
The bride gets to decide what she wants today. It's *her* day.

Of course, I doubt that any bride would wear a crystal-beaded, duchess satin gown or a long cathedral train on the beach on a hot summer day. And does the bride getting married at a summer wedding in a garden or the park really want to drag a full beaded train across the grass? Surely not!

Comfort and practicality should be an important consideration in both cases.

Brides should be aware that while modern fashion sensibilities won't put restrictions on gown choices anymore, places of worship might. Before making a purchase, make sure off-the-shoulder styles and plunging necklines and nude dresses aren't no-nos at your ceremony site.

Which brings me back to the subject of your venue and where exactly you will be married. No dress decisions should be made until you have made this decision and booked your venue.

So, what do you have in mind? Do you want your wedding closer to home, or would you rather have a destination wedding?

Formal or informal?

Traditional or trendy?

Chapel or cathedral?

Winter or summer?

Day or night?

Far away or closer to home?

Casual, outdoor?

Beach or garden?

So many decisions to make!

Then, there is the venue to consider. There are myriad options to choose from when deciding on a venue.

Where would you like to have your wedding?

Do you prefer a barefoot vibe, or do you always imagine yourself as a bride in a grand ballroom?

What theme should your wedding have? If you adore a certain time period, have your wedding reflect it. One of the couples I worked with turned their nuptials into a medieval-inspired affair.

Okay—yes, sure you would love to one-up your friend, sister, or third cousin who just had a super-lavish wedding. You see them planning ceremonies on beaches, mountaintops, castles, gold-plated banquet halls, picturesque shanties, and you want your wedding to be just as, if not more, spectacular.

Your purse may not be overflowing like theirs, so don't let tears make an appearance when you get that final credit card bill. You want your wedding to be an occasion of pure joy, not the gateway to bankruptcy.

But, no matter what you decide, your wedding deserves a legendary setting.

From a barefoot beach ceremony and a glamorous seaside reception under the stars to cocktails served on the beach and sunset vows with a private firework display, to a mountaintop ski resort, a destination wedding need not be an expensive, clichéd affair. Depending on your taste and budget, there are numerous choices available.

Planned properly, destination weddings can be quite appealing to budget-conscious couples, as packages generally include all of the details, from decorations and seating to your bouquet, cake, dinner, drinks, and the honeymoon suite, as well as rooms for guests, suite upgrades, and services like massages, plus your taxes and gratuities, all of which you would otherwise need to pay for separately.

A destination wedding is ideal for guests based in different cities, as they can all stay on one property with the convenience of knowing that all details will be taken care of. At the same time, guests can enjoy the resort's services and amenities. Selecting an all-inclusive resort for your wedding gives you the freedom to enjoy your events without the hassle of worrying about the nitty-gritty details that would normally be taken care of by you or a dedicated wedding coordinator. This ensures that all expectations for your wedding are realized.

Each venue offers different options for personalizing the ceremony and reception, so make sure to communicate your wishes clearly early on. In most cases, you can request to add personal touches to your special day, with live music, photo packages, and special lighting and effects, fireworks—even a signature cocktail.

Typically, a destination wedding lasts three days, allowing enough time for rehearsal, the wedding, and plenty of downtime so that you and your guests can relax and truly enjoy your time together. Guests and the wedding party usually pay for their own travel and accommodations. However, it is not uncommon for the bride and groom to pick up the tab for special family members.

Considering the guests are dedicating a weekend to you and paying for travel and accommodations, it is best not to expect wedding gifts from them.

If you are planning a destination wedding, here are some steps to take:

1. ***Research resorts in your country/location of choice:*** Choose one that speaks to your wedding vision as a couple. Visit the property you have in mind in advance in order to fully experience the venue before making your decision.

2. ***Set a budget:*** Detail what you can realistically afford. Research airfare, and factor in the number of guests and resort room rates. Don't forget to factor in incidentals and overtime charges, especially if you will be using the services of outside vendors such as photographers, florists, and musicians. Make sure to include the following in your budget:

    - A pre-wedding trip to check out the venue
    - A welcome party
    - Welcome gift bags
    - At least one group activity
    - Rehearsal dinner

- Reception
- Morning-after brunch
- Airport shuttle to and from the resort for guests
- Your own transportation to and from the resort

3. ***Gather your ideas:*** Consider color schemes and venue backdrop, details, and concepts you would like reflected in your wedding.

4. ***Meet the property's wedding coordinator:*** This person can guide you through the ins and outs of the resort. Taste the cuisine, check out the rooms and suites, and go over the style and colors of your theme to showcase your unique style with everything from flowers to lighting, photographer, and music.

5. ***Notify family and friends***: Let them know your decision and set a date that works for all.

6. ***Look into the marriage legalities in the country/location where you would like to be married:*** Depending on your destination, you may need to meet with local consulates and bring documents such as birth certificates, passports, and, if applicable, divorce decrees to be notarized, translated, and/or apostilled. It can take a while to receive your marriage certificate in the US, so you will not be able to do a name change or receive spousal benefits until you have the document. Ask your on-site wedding coordinator to help you navigate paperwork on her end. If you don't have a wedding planner, check the State Department website (travel.state.gov) for more information and legalities on the country in which you're getting married.

7. ***Have a Plan B ready:*** Take into consideration the season, as Mother Nature can be the worst wedding crasher of them all. Many couples find themselves stuck without a heat wave or rain plan and fall short on making guests feel comfortable outdoors. Also, vendors might be unable to deliver because of logistical

snafus. Have a Plan B ready just in case. If having an outdoor wedding, make alternate arrangements for indoor venue should you have to move at the last minute.

8. ***Consider access to the location:*** Have all arrangements in place. For example, if the location is up on a hill or in the middle of a field, consider how your guests can get there, especially elderly or differently abled guests who may find it difficult to navigate by foot or drive so far. Arrange alternate transportation to make everyone's commute to the site and back easier. Check whether the venue allows for handicapped access.

9. ***Get wedding and/or travel insurance:*** Many major insurance companies offer wedding-specific plans tailored to your individual needs, which can include vendor no-shows, attire mishaps, jewelry loss, illness, and weather, as well as out-of-country claims. Travel insurance can cover cancellations due to weather or other unforeseen complications such as airline strike, illness, baggage loss, and overseas medical care.

10. ***Send save-the-dates:*** Put together your guest list and send out save-the-dates to give your guests plenty of time to make travel and other arrangements.

11. ***Reserve guest rooms:*** Once you have all RSVPs from guests, reserve a block of rooms.

12. ***Set up a wedding website:*** This is where you can post your wedding date and convey every piece of your wedding information so guests can access everything from location, travel information, and lodging options, as well as group activities and events you have planned for them. Make sure to update this regularly to include your most recent information.

13. ***Book early:*** Begin planning early and book ahead to save on airfare. If your wedding will take place in another country, ask

your travel agent about reserving a block of seats with an airline. Many carriers offer discounts to passengers with groups over ten.

14. **Apply/renew travel documents:** If you need to apply for or renew passports, you should start the process as soon as you have your venue.

15. **Simplify:** Fly direct rather than cramming in stop-overs, as it can be quite stressful. Besides, the chances of your luggage being lost or delayed are slim to none on direct flights.

16. **Pack your gown well:** If you plan on carrying your gown on board, pack it well. Aim to have everything packed and ready to carry about one week before your departure. Have your salon pack your dress and veil in a garment bag to avoid excessive wrinkling, so you can easily hand-carry it onto the plane. Do NOT—I repeat, do not—check your wedding dress with your luggage. Call and inform the airline in advance that you'll be carrying your attire, and once on board, ask the flight attendant to carefully store your garment bag, preferably hanging it in a closet near your seat.

17. **Consider concierge services:** For honeymoons abroad, you can book all transportation via concierge services that have extensive networks, instead of worrying about how to coordinate in far-flung locales. These companies will tend to your service preferences with "white-glove service" so you and your guests feel like celebs!

18. **Ship what you can:** Ship gift bag items, printed materials such as programs, your wedding dress (if not hand-carrying it on board) and groom's attire, and all accessories to the site. Address the parcel to the attention of your on-site wedding coordinator. Some items, such as medication and liquors, can get hung up at

customs, so do the proper research about the rules that apply and make sure to use a reputable importer/exporter service to ensure safe and timely arrival.

19. **Finalize and confirm:** Finalize your seating plan, determine the photo schedule and shot list for the photographer, give the caterer your final guest list count, and go over all the logistics with your wedding coordinator again. Do a walk-through of the property for another look at your ceremony and reception locations.

20. **Prepare welcome gift bags:** Include a welcome letter, contact information for a point person or two for help with any questions that may come up, and an itinerary of events in your gift bags. Distribute them to guests' rooms.

21. **Share information with guests:** Communicate with your guests on what they can expect. List details such as weather changes if the wedding will take place outdoors. Let them know so they are prepared to wear sunglasses for the day and wraps for the evening.

22. **Prepare your attire:** Steam your dress and the groom's tuxedo. Have a hair and makeup run-through with your veil or headpiece.

23. **Get plenty of rest:** And try not to overindulge at the rehearsal dinner, so you can feel refreshed and look your best on your wedding day.

24. **Pause:** Leave a day between your wedding and your honeymoon to relax.

Many brides choose to honeymoon at the same resort where they get married. After all, why leave paradise after the wedding?

WHAT TO WEAR?

When choosing what to wear, always keep your location and climate in mind.

Your wedding dress and the venue are two mutually inclusive factors that affect your overall wedding theme. Once you have chosen your venue, you can focus on the style of your dress. Pick one that is practical and convenient for the location.

On the Beach: The fun and casual vibe of the sandy shores makes for a dream venue for a wedding. Your dress should be of lightweight fabric that packs well and doesn't wrinkle easily. Styles without excessive beading are best for a tropical locale or beach wedding. Think comfort and match the casual ambiance with a simpler choice that is quirky and not typical bridal fare. Forgo a too-long train or a veil length that may blow around in the breeze. Fabrics such as silk tulle, organza, chiffon, silk charmeuse, georgette or light laces, loosely gathered ruffles, and flowy fabrics are ideal for a beach wedding. Your dress should be comfortable and flatter your figure. Sheaths, mermaids, A-lines, short dresses, and cocktail-length dresses are all appropriate, as long as they are in the right fabrics. You may choose tropical hues, such as bright turquoise or coral accents, in your jewelry. Hair combs and fresh flowers in your hair to complement your gown and shoes such as low-heeled wedges or flat sandals that allow you to walk on sand or uneven ground should all be considered.

On a Cruise: A cruise is a great way to have a destination wedding. It can be very affordable and does wonders for keeping romance afloat. Your best bet is to splurge on a suite with a balcony so you can spend time alone under the stars. With the nautical and oceanic backdrop, your gown should have some special feature to make it stand out, such as embellishments and ruffles for drama. Sparkling details in crystal and metal and fluttering ruffles in the skirt are perfect complements to the beauty of the seascape around you. Think light and airy fabrics. Keep the dress volume narrow and keep embellishments to a minimum. The ideal silhouettes for a cruise wedding are flowing sheaths and A-lines in fabrics that drape well such as luxurious silk satin, silk charmeuse, and soft chiffon.

YOUR BRIDAL STYLE

In the Country or at the Park: Have a fairy-tale wedding in the countryside or at the park with nature as your backdrop. Lush green surroundings with the sweet scents of a beautiful garden venue create a romantic ambience. Light, airy wedding dresses in breathable fabrics like lightweight silk, chiffon and gossamer lace, with hemlines at the ankle or above, with pretty floral motifs, are fabulous for a spring or summer wedding. If marrying in autumn or winter, choose a dress made from thicker fabrics such as velvet or wool blends, perhaps with sleeves to stay warm. Add an accessory such as a cape or a shrug, or even a stylish bolero jacket. A wedding gown with a long train would be impractical and inconvenient for sure. Shoes should be comfortable to allow you to walk on uneven terrain. Kitten heels, peep-toes, and sandals are ideal, or make a statement with unusual options like boots or sneakers. The feeling should be casual and relaxed.

In the City Hall: There are no hard-and-fast rules if you will be saying "I do" at the City Hall. You can be as fashionable as you like, as modern or as traditional as you can get. Your dress should stand out and make you look and feel like the bride that you are. Your outfit can be smart but dressy, or smart and minimalist, preferably with a shorter or no train. You could wear a colored wedding dress, perhaps with sheer cap sleeves and even a little glitter. A whimsical lacy sheer-legged pantsuit is a great option! Be ladylike and liberal.

YOUR BRIDAL STYLE

At a Church or in a Place of Worship: Check with your chosen venue on rules you as the bride may be expected to follow if marrying in a place of worship. Many traditional religious venues expect modesty and do not encourage revealing dress styles including strapless or sheer bodices. You may choose a dress with cap sleeves or longer sleeves, or opt to wear a bolero or jacket for the ceremony over a strapless dress to conform to the rules if necessary. An illusion neckline is modest and stylish as well as classic. As the wedding is formal in nature, your dress can be lavish with a long, majestic train, and paired with traditional accessories like a veil to make a huge impact and stand out among the crowd. Luxurious fabrics like duchess satin and pure silk or elegant and rich lace are all suitable. Ball gowns are extremely popular for traditional church weddings, as are A-lines and mermaid styles. Details and beautiful embellishments such as intricate embroidery and beading are all suitable and bound to impress.

At a Resort: Think champagne toasts in picturesque gardens, a lavish ceremony in a grand ballroom. Luxe, intimate ambiance and impressive views of the skyline, all perfect for your magical day and for bringing your unique vision to life and fulfilling your every desire. Most resorts have extravagant ballrooms designed for lavish weddings. The style, sophistication, and elegance of a luxury resort calls for a dress that is fashionable and majestic. Based on the theme and formality of your venue you can opt for any silhouette that suits your fancy. The choice is yours as you have more flexibility here than at a place of worship. From modern silhouettes such as fit-and-flare styles, body-skimming sheaths, and A-lines to extravagant ball gowns or even minimalistic and uncluttered, snug-fitting silhouettes—anything goes. Fabrics can be duchess satin, vintage-inspired lace, or airy fabrics such as tulle and lightweight silk charmeuse. Go for rich details, tasteful embellishments that refine and add a touch of sophistication and lend a touch of elegance. For your reception in the gardens, you could change into a simpler style, even a short dress—easier to dance into the night.

In the Desert: Rustic venues set in the desert are intimate, warm, and cozy with a relaxed and laid-back ambiance. Your dress style should reflect your backdrop. You could wear a vintage-inspired lace or chiffon dress in a simple, relaxed silhouette that is not too fitted, such as an A-line or a sheath, a short or tea-length dress, with minimalistic details and embellishments. Boho wedding dresses and those with ample lace details conjure up nostalgia and add a vintage charm. Your dress must have the right balance of details without being overwhelming or too elaborate. A birdcage veil will add to the vintage charm and complete the look.

At a Castle: A castle can bring alive a fairy-tale vibe, characterized by magnificent old-world décor, perhaps with domed ceilings and courtyard entry and picture-perfect views. You can go "glamping" in castle vineyards with an equally impressive style. Typically formal, a castle wedding is characterized by magnificent décor. A princess-style gown, a traditional ball gown drenched in heavy layers of tulle and organza, and classic details such as lace, beaded, or crystal embroidery add plenty of sparkle and drama to an already grand and stately setting. Or, go all out in a fairy-tale inspired Mikado or pure silk dress with long sleeves and a high neck that is simple yet romantic with old-world elegance. A dress that fully covers you creates a sense of purity and mystery.

At Home: Your dream wedding can be held in your own backyard, where the grills are glowing and hurricane lamps are flickering under a big white tent. This is an ideal setting, especially if you have the space and are on a budget while having a wedding that is unique to you, one that has a warm and intimate feel. Transform your garden into a gorgeous gazebo-esque venue, or commission a leafy bower to be made as your backdrop which can be your focal point, an intimate spot to hold a blessing. Silky satin and Alençon lace with soft and feminine elements look fresh and romantic and are best in the natural greenery. Your dress should be both practical and comfortable. Avoid dresses with long trains. Choose a dress that hangs well, especially if it gets windy. Dresses with some beading around the hem qualifies or else have your seamstress sew small weights into the hem of your dress so it always falls nicely and doesn't flail around in the wind. A short bouffant veil adds a touch of glamour to your overall look.

Trendy: For a trendy, laid-back feel, the setting can be a downtown loft, the wine room of a hot new restaurant, or the atrium of a contemporary art museum. Tall pillars evoke awe, and votive candles can be arranged in tight groupings, illuminating tables of long-stem flowers arranged in tall glass vases, with outstanding cuisine, artistic presentation, and impeccable service by the culinary team to help make you feel pampered and special. The ideal wedding dress would be something strapless and sexy, or short and chic, in silk charmeuse or French lace with ankle-tie sandals.

THEMED WEDDINGS

A themed wedding seems to be more popular nowadays especially among younger couples, as it encompasses what both bride and groom are drawn to, representing their likes and passions.

Get carried away with a theme that is based on your favorite comic or a genre such as Superheroes, Star Wars, or even Independence Day. Feel free to expand on your creative side and inject a unique message into your wedding décor. Think out of the box!

Below are some ideas:

Independence Day: We had a bride who got married in Las Vegas on Independence Day and had her gown made in the colors of our flag. She walked down the aisle in a deep-red-colored Thai silk ball gown, embroidered with white- and blue-thread floral motifs and tri-color Swarovski crystal beading. Her fiancé wore a white shirt under a navy-blue suit with a custom-embroidered cummerbund and bow tie to match the embroidery on his bride's dress. Place cards in colors of the flag and white-covered chairs tied in the back with huge tri-color ribbons adorned the room. Rose petals in red, white, and blue were strewn down the aisle. Definitely festive!

Superhero: Your love of comics can be incorporated into your wedding day in various forms, such as having the groomsmen wear your favorite superhero shirt underneath their tuxedos or wear themed cuff links. Bridesmaids could even hold bouquets made from comic book pages. Action figures holding nameplates, comical invitation cards, and even colorful wedding favors for the guests would look fabulous!

Winter Wonderland: Perfect for a winter wedding where you can use pinecones, berries, or evergreen boughs as ornaments to adorn church pews and chairs. You and your bridesmaids can wear faux fur stoles and be transported in horse-drawn sleighs to a cozy cottage decorated in silver and cool blues with shimmering crystals to give an icy effect for your reception.

So many choices await. Go out and write your story on the sands or on the mountaintops that have launched over a century of love stories. No doubt your wedding day will be one of the most unforgettable days in your life, one that will be remembered by your near and dear ones for years to come.

Be adventurous. Be unique. Be you.

Launch your own Love Story

Chapter Four

YOUR WEDDING BUDGET

First comes love, then comes marriage, which includes wedding expenses . . .

Let's face it: Getting married is not cheap. According to a recent study, weddings cost an average of $35,329 nationally.

As you begin to ponder all-important decisions about your dress, floral arrangements, cake fillings, photographer, food, music, etc., be realistic and take a step back to decide how much you can really afford to spend on your big day. Before you lock in the final details of your wedding day, prioritize which elements are most important to you.

Certainly, it can be tough reaching a compromise as you prepare your guest list and plan your menu and your venue, the dress you would absolutely love to wear for your walk down the aisle, the band you want to play at your wedding. Don't feel obligated to please others or feel tied to old-fashioned etiquette. You're not obligated to spend that much, and many couples don't. Set a reasonable budget and cut costs on some of the most expensive elements of your nuptials. After all, you do not want to start your marriage in debt.

Unlike days past, where the bride's family would take care of the full cost of the ceremony and reception with the groom picking up the cost of the rings and the honeymoon, today it is more likely that you and your other half are jointly footing the bill, or splitting the costs three ways between your families and you as a couple.

A financial conversation, although sometimes tough and uncomfortable to have, is important so that you will know exactly what your capacity is, how much you can work with, and how much each will need to contribute to make the wedding happen. It also opens the door for the couple to talk about post-wedding matters like shared or separate checking accounts and life insurance, among other matters.

First off, take a careful look at what aspects of your wedding will cost you the most and decide which areas mean the most to you so you can allocate your funds accordingly.

Create a budget worksheet to include the following:

- Wedding coordinator
- Reception
- Wedding rings
- Honeymoon
- Wedding gown and accessories (veil, slip, shoes, undergarments)
- Wedding gown alterations
- Hair and makeup
- Bridesmaids' gifts
- Bridesmaids' luncheon
- Ceremony

Groom's attire and accessories

Groomsmen's gifts

Officiant's fee

Photography

Videography

Prenuptial agreement

Rehearsal dinner

Wedding cake

Wedding day transportation

Wedding favors

Ceremony and rehearsal music

Flowers

Invitations and stationery

Marriage license

Medical tests

Wedding night suite

Write down who will pay for what and the estimated costs of each item. Visit possible locations to compare prices and make sure to include sales tax, gratuities, and overtime fees to your estimates. Ask about payment policies and deposits required to lock in your dates. Make sure to get all details in

writing and have the vendors include the dates, times, prices, and descriptions of all services they will provide.

Wedding budgets generally get divided as such:

Reception: 40%

Honeymoon: 15%

Photography/Videography: 10%

Bridal Apparel: 8%

Engagement/wedding rings: 7%

Music: 5%

Flowers: 5%

Invitations: 2%

Miscellaneous (attendants' gifts, rehearsal dinner, ceremony fees, transportation, etc.): 8%

Here are twenty-five smart tips on how you can save on costs as you plan your wedding:

1. ***Skip Saturday:*** This is the most popular and expensive day for weddings. To save money, consider holding your wedding on a Sunday, or even a weeknight instead.
2. ***Consider the morning or afternoon:*** You'll be able to save on the menu as morning and afternoon weddings call for lighter, less expensive fare.
3. ***Choose a less popular month:*** You'll usually pay a higher price for a venue during the most popular seasons: spring and summer. Consider a winter wedding instead, like January or February, months when you could easily score a discount.

4. *Negotiate the venue's resources:* Unexpected expenses can pop up, including corkage fees, cake-cutting, and power for your DJ and photo booth. Some venues charge for the rental of tables and linens if you opt for a backyard wedding. If you find this unreasonable, ask that these line items be removed. Read the venue's contract in its entirety before signing.

5. *Have your officiant perform your ceremony at the reception:* This option will help you avoid paying for an additional location fee and save your guests the travel.

6. *Purchase your gown online or during a sale:* There are more gowns available now than ever before, and you have plenty of options to find a gorgeous dress you can afford. Browse online to purchase, or ask the bridal store in your area when they're having a sale or a trunk show during which times designers offer incentives and special pricing.

7. *Something borrowed:* Rather than purchasing your accessories, such as veil, jewelry, and shoes, borrow these items from friends and family.

8. *Choose in-season blooms:* You can save a bundle by picking flowers that are in season at the time of your wedding. Note that loose-cut flowers are less expensive than sculpted centerpieces; hand-tied stems are more affordable than carefully constructed bouquets; and larger flowers naturally look fuller and take up more space with fewer stems.

9. *Repurpose your flowers:* You can repurpose ceremony flowers for the reception instead of spending money on buying more. For instance, use

a ceremony arch to adorn your sweetheart table at the reception.

10. ***Save on the décor:*** Your floral designer may have excess inventory they are willing to part with or lend out for free. Your recently married friends may have table centerpieces or other items left over that you could borrow. Just ask. Also check out craft stores for wedding decorations to save on costs.

11. ***Tone down your guest list***: Be mindful of your budget when drawing up your guest list. Choose a more elaborate experience for a smaller set of guests who really matter to you, rather than inviting every acquaintance you have ever met. Also, not everyone needs to receive an invite with a "plus one."

12. ***Save on photography***: Limit your photographer's hours. You may need them for the ceremony, but perhaps not for the reception. One way to get the extra pictures is to give each table of reception guests a disposable camera with which to take candid shots that they can upload on an online photo-sharing site.

13. ***Save on videography***: Book your videography services as part of a package to include microphone rentals, editing, additional tape copies, and enough hours to cover your entire wedding so you don't get hit with overtime charges.

14. ***Get a big-band sound without the expense:*** Music sets the tone for your wedding and reception. If possible, hire the same musicians to perform at both the ceremony and the reception. Hire a smaller band, since most bands charge per musician. If your ceremony will be held in a place of worship, you may

be able to use their regular musicians at minimal expense.

15. ***Save on invitations:*** Choose thermography (a less expensive printing process) over pricey engraved invitations. Eliminate inserts. Reception details can be printed on the lower part of the invitation instead. Traditional invitations can be mailed, but wedding itineraries can be posted on your wedding website, and save-the-date alerts can be sent via email.

16. ***Save on the groom's attire:*** Rent rather than buy. Many formal wear rental places provide the groom's tux for a discount or for free if the rest of the groomsmen rent their formal wear there. Look for package deals.

17. ***Food and liquor:*** A wedding brunch or lunch is less costly than a traditional formal dinner. Or, if you prefer a sit-down plated meal, then opt for a three-course over a five-course meal. Minimize the cost of your bar tab by opting for shooters. Cut down on drink sizes. Have your signature drinks served in smaller glasses, as most people will take a sip to try the signature drink and then go back to their regular drinks.

18. ***Your cake:*** The cake you cut for your pictures doesn't have to be the one that feeds all your guests. The more tiers on your cake, the more it will cost you. Go for a shorter cake with fewer tiers and have sheet cakes in the back to be cut up and served. Your guests will not notice the difference.

19. **Wedding rings:** Note that 14-karat gold bands are less expensive than 18-karat gold, and white gold can provide the same look as platinum for a lot less.

20. **Transportation savings:** Most limousine companies charge per car, per hour. Just one limo can take care of all your transportation needs, taking you and your bridesmaids to the ceremony, and then you and your groom, best man, and maid of honor to the reception. You can also rent a luxury car like a Lincoln town car or a Cadillac for the whole day for less.

21. **Save on pre-wedding parties:** Host a luncheon or rehearsal dinner at your or your parents' home instead of a restaurant. It is more intimate and will help cut down on costs.

22. **Hire a day-of wedding coordinator:** If hiring a full-time wedding planner does not fit your budget but you feel coordinating your wedding is too stressful, you could consider hiring a wedding coordinator just for the day of your wedding to help supervise the festivities and oversee the itinerary so your carefully planned details are not forgotten.

23. **Hair and makeup budgeting:** Rather than have your stylist come to your house, you could go to her salon instead. Seek out a professional who can do both hair and makeup so you don't have to pay two people.

24. **Honeymoon savings:** Consider a honeymoon during the off-season to save on flights and accommodations. Most hotels offer honeymoon packages that include free champagne and breakfast as well as special discounts for spa treatments.

25. ***Use a credit card with travel awards:*** Use your credit card to pay for everything, but make sure to use it responsibly. Don't take on more debt than you can afford to pay off. The accumulated points can be used toward your honeymoon.

Starting your marriage in debt is always the wrong thing to do, so don't get talked into spending more than you can afford. Don't cave in to vendor attempts to upsell you.

Make adjustments and cut out unnecessary expenses in the months leading to the wedding so you can bulk up your savings.

Above all, be realistic when planning your budget. Set realistic spending limits from the very beginning that account for all areas of your wedding. If you overspend in one area, cut back in another and keep adjusting to stay within your budget.

Say "I don't" to debt.

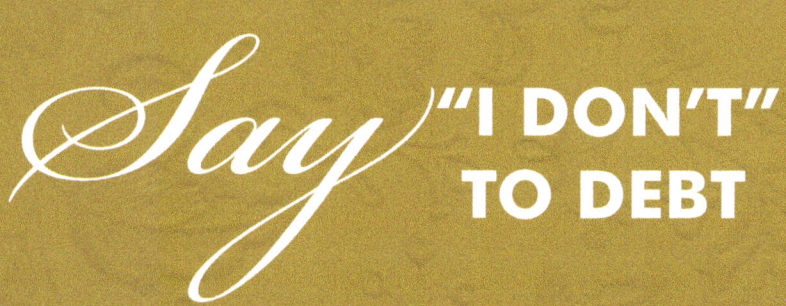

Chapter Five

LINES THAT FLATTER:
Choosing a Style for Your Figure

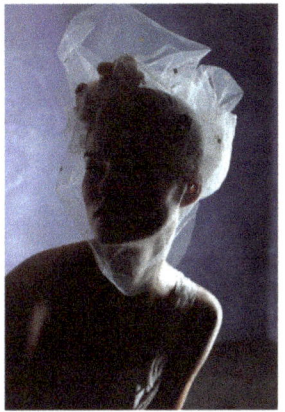

Say what? There are actually some styles that will look better on me than others?

Yes, that's right.

Marrying your soul mate is easy, but now comes the hard part: finding the right dress to suit your body.

While true beauty radiates from the inside, choosing a gown that flatters your body type is an important step on the road to your own personal body of style.

Your wedding dress is much more than fabric and beading—it encompasses and celebrates your dreams and aspirations, and should be just as perfectly beautiful and as beautifully perfect. So be realistic about your body shape, but don't be too hard on yourself, because there is a wedding dress ideal for your shape and size, made specifically to enhance and beautify your form—a fantasy wrapped in fabric, made just for you.

There are a lot of descriptions to consider and apply to the perfect wedding dress. Your dream dress depends on your personality, the kind of wedding you will have, the venue and time of year, and whether the event is formal or informal, small or large.

Before you stress and drive yourself nuts over trains and veils, necklines and waistlines, and all of the parts of the body you feel you have to hide, there's one thing you have to know: All brides—I repeat, *all* brides—are beautiful.

I understand this step can be overwhelming and suggest you give yourself a break from being too critical. You are beautiful just as you are.

Now I invite you to get in front of the mirror and write down the things about your body that you like. Yes, seriously. Please do so . . .

Then honestly, but not mercilessly, turn to the areas that you are not so gung-ho about, where a well-placed pleat or a wisp of illusion may help you feel self-assured. This will make your next step easier.

To help, I've explained what works (and what doesn't) for different figure silhouettes in this chapter. I've taken all the mystery out of finding your dream dress—and left in all the magic.

Highlighting five common body shapes, I will help you see which is the closest one you belong to, and then figure out which neckline, silhouette, and fabric works best for you. No matter what shape or size, I've got you covered!

To help you select the best wedding dress for your body shape, I've laid out some guidelines here. My advice is specific; the details small but crucial. With notes in hand, you will be better equipped to start shopping for the dress of your dreams, one that gives you the confidence you deserve.

You may, of course, feel inclined to ignore some of the guidelines, and that is perfectly fine, so long as you know your strengths and dress according to your body shape.

But first, we need to determine what your body shape is.

There are five basic female body types, and each of us falls closer to one than the others. There are, in fact, some styles you would do better to avoid and others that would enhance your figure.

The simplest way to identify your body type is by measuring your bust, waist, and hips in this manner:

Bust: Wearing a properly fitting bra, run the measuring tape behind your back and measure the circumference of your bust at the widest point.

Waist: With your stomach relaxed, measure the circumference of your waist at the narrowest point.

Hips: Standing straight, measure the circumference of your hips at the widest point.

Now you are ready to compare these three measurements against the five most common body shapes to identify which body type you belong to. You can also use an online calculator by going to www.calculator.net/body-type-calculator. It will give you a general idea of the body type you fall under.

All women lean toward one of these basic shapes, but only a few of us will be exactly one of these. For instance, if your bust or waist changes or if you feel bloated, you may get different results.

Ready? Let's explore . . .

DIFFERENT BODY TYPES

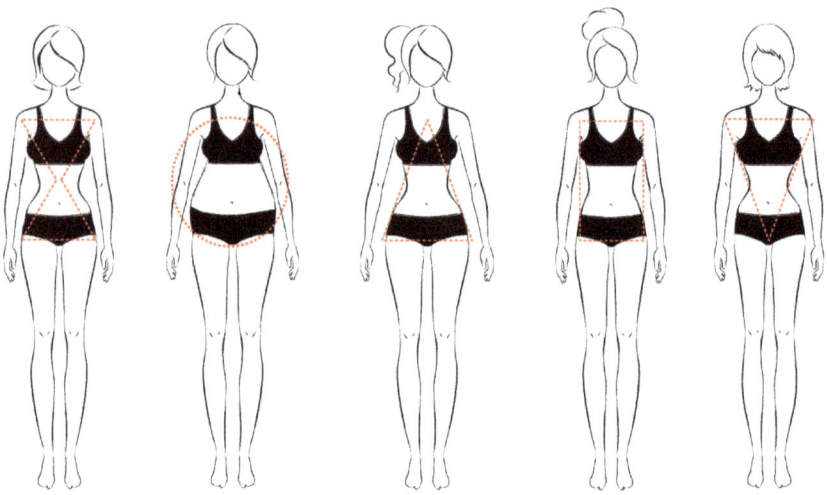

What are the most flattering silhouettes for your figure?

What tricks do you need to know that will help highlight your best features and downplay those that are of concern to you?

Camouflaging those concerns is a study in itself. Empowering yourself with that knowledge will help you achieve the overall look you wish to express on your most important day.

Whether you are pear-shaped or petite, top-heavy or tall, each bride is looking for a dress that will enhance her figure. And to do this, you need help.

A woman's figure falls under one of the following categories:

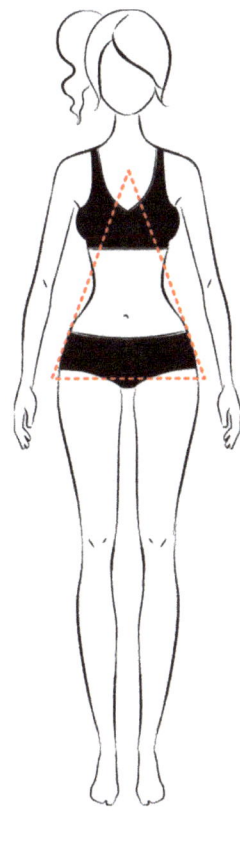

Pear

PEAR/TRIANGLE:
Smaller on the top and heavier on the bottom.

Described as the most "curvaceous" body type. You are bottom-heavy with hips that are wider than your shoulders. Fat tends to accumulate on your thighs and sometimes the buttocks. Therefore, your lower body—hips, thighs, and sometimes your behind—are more noticeable. Your shoulders are narrower, sloping, and not as broad. You tend to have an elongated waist and your legs tend to be shorter and are noticeably wider, muscular, and fuller compared to the rest of your body.

To balance the proportions, your dress should have elements that will broaden and emphasize the top and de-emphasize the hips. To achieve this, padded shoulders, pouf sleeves, half- or full-sleeve treatments, or an off-the-shoulder look that will extend the shoulder lines are recommended. A bodice adorned with lace, dimensional beadwork, and appliques will add texture and help draw the focus upward and broaden the top portion, helping accentuate a narrow waistline.

Recommend: A-lines; mermaids; empires; ball gowns.

Avoid: Fitted, body-hugging sheaths; narrow or set-in sleeves; extra-full skirts.

THE INVERTED TRIANGLE:
Fuller on the top and narrower on the bottom.

You are top-heavy—broader on the top and narrower on the bottom. You usually wear a larger size on top. Your shoulders are wider and broader, your hips narrower. Your bust tends to be proportionately large. Your waist is a few inches smaller than your hips, and your legs are usually slimmer.

The idea is to de-emphasize the top and shoulders while giving more volume and adding width to the lower half. This can be achieved by selecting gowns with simpler bodices with little or no accents, natural shoulder lines, moderate or no padding, and set-in sleeves. At the same time, skirts can be full, or have details such as bustles and peplums, as these will give balance to the overall look.

Recommend: A-lines; empires; ball gowns.

Avoid: Mermaids; sheaths; bodices with empire waistlines or plunging necklines; gowns with full sleeves.

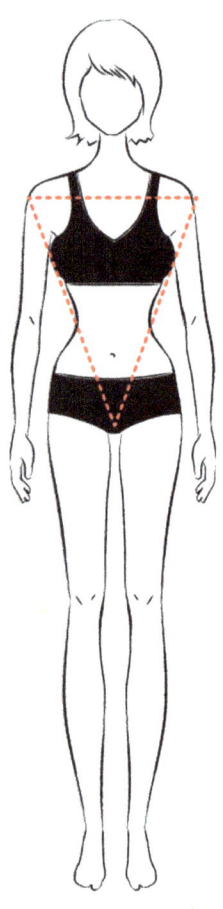

Inverted Triangle

RULER:
Straight-up-and-down proportions with very little waist definition.

Also described as straight/rectangular, the ruler has a "boyish" profile and may have a thin body that tends to lack curves. Your hips tend to have a similar width as your shoulders. Your waist measures about the same as your bust and hips. You do not notice any significant curves around the waist area and there is no waist definition. Your bust tends to be small or average. You look fairly straight-up with flat shoulders.

The idea is to create curves in the right places. The bodice can have oversized shoulders and sleeves, as well as horizontal detailing, all of which will add width while giving the illusion of a narrower waist.

Recommend: A-lines; empires; ball gowns; sheaths.

Avoid: Mermaids; body-clinging fabrics; slim skirts.

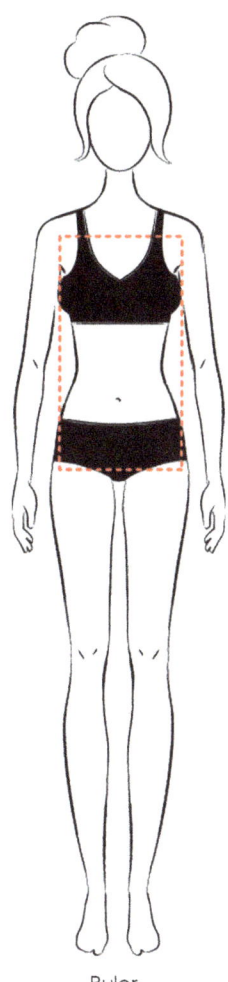
Ruler

YOUR BRIDAL STYLE

HOURGLASS:
Full bust and full hips
with waist definition.

Your hips and bust are usually equal, with a well-defined, narrow waist. Fat is generally stored evenly throughout. Your curves are flattering, although you may still have fleshy upper arms and wide-looking shoulders.

With your full hips and bust and a narrow waist you can wear pretty much any silhouette! Strapless, off the shoulder, and V-necklines all complement your figure.

Recommend: Mermaids; A-lines; empires; ball gowns; sheaths.

Avoid: Too much ornamentation and details on bodices; pouf sleeves.

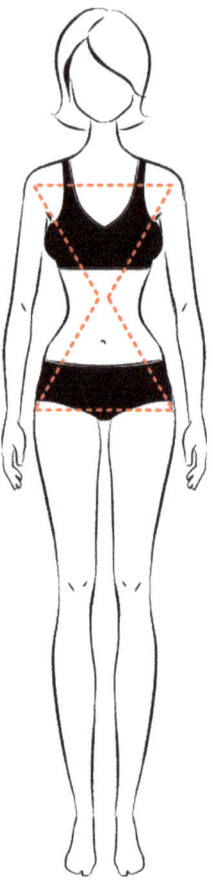

Hourglass

APPLE/ROUND:
Full bust and full hips,
without waist definition.

Your bust is a few inches larger than your hips. Your weight is concentrated around your mid-section and chest, sometimes giving the illusion of a bigger bust and a protruding stomach. Your waistline has little definition, and you are top-heavy. Your legs tend to be slimmer. Wide shoulders and slim limbs, especially the arms, are the usual characteristics of this body type.

Recommend: A-lines; empires.

Avoid: Mermaids; sheaths; ball gowns; fabrics and ornamentations that will overpower your figure.

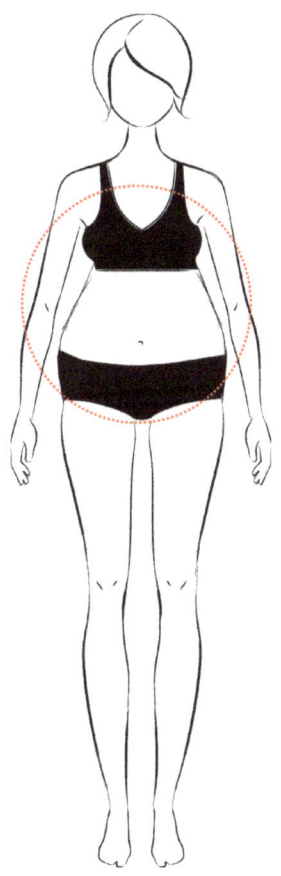

Apple

OTHER CONSIDERATIONS

If you are . . .

Petite: You have a smaller stature and are shorter than average. Camouflage this by choosing gowns that will appear to lengthen and elongate the torso and add height. Go with vertical lines and patterns. Beading that goes linear from head to toe makes you look taller.

- ***Recommend***: Column-like sheaths; A-lines; moderately full skirts with minimal or no details; bodices with natural waistlines; vertical details; and simple or no sleeves. Stick to open, sexier necklines—think strapless and off-the-shoulder styles, as they give you more body length. Concentrate details like beading or lacework above the hemline.

- ***Avoid***: Voluminous ball gowns; pouf skirts; cathedral trains; thick fabrics; dropped waistlines.

Tall: Height can be an asset, but there must be the right balance between length and leanness and volume.

- ***Recommend:*** A soft ball gown without too much fullness in the skirt is best; a skirt shape that is flat in the front with details such as draping or bustles in the back.

- ***Avoid:*** High necklines; long sleeves; big, pouf dresses, as they can be overpowering; very slim dresses, which can make you look even taller.

Full-figured/Plus-size: You have a significantly curvaceous figure with body proportions that tend to be larger than average.

- ***Recommend:*** A-line and sheath dresses with empire waistlines or those that cinch at the thinnest part of the waist; satin fabric; Basque waist; sweetheart or V-necklines with details which will help draw the eye upward; A-line skirts to help camouflage the hips; short or three-quarter-length fitted sleeves to help slenderize arms.

- ***Avoid:*** Mermaids; slim sheaths; body-hugging skirts; slinky bias-cut dresses; dresses that drape loosely, as they add extra pounds to the overall look; extremely full skirts; strapless or sleeveless gowns.

OTHER DO'S AND DON'TS

If you are . . .

Thick-waisted: Volume in the skirt helps create a waist that looks small by contrast. Seaming can also help trick the eye. If the vertical seams are placed close together at the waist then fan out, it tends to make you look smaller because the eye focuses on the vertical lines. An empire waistline is flattering, as is a corseted bodice.

Short-waisted: Look for a dropped waistline or one that angles downward into a V, such as a Basque waist, that will help elongate your torso. Narrow silhouettes and bias cuts create length. Wearing princess-style dresses will elongate and lengthen the torso, while an empire waist draws the eye away from the area.

Long-waisted: Avoid dropped waists as they make your upper body look longer than necessary. To de-emphasize the long torso, wear a style that has a higher waistline such as an empire style or one that hits just below the empire, which is also flattering, with either an A-line skirt or a straight skirt. The horizontal emphasis of a strapless style can also help.

If you have . . .

Full hips: A-line skirts are best, as they keep you looking lean and long, but you must be strategic about where the skirt starts and the bodice ends. Moderately full skirts without bustles, ruffles, and bows also work well.

Big bust: Open necklines are the most flattering, so opt for an off-the-shoulder bodice or portrait, scoop, sweetheart, or V-necklines with minimal detailing. Pick a dress with a smooth line that doesn't have a very defined waist, such as a princess-line dress, which is the most flattering because it has plenty of vertical lines and doesn't break the body in half and serves to de-emphasize the bust. Strapless usually pushes the bust up too much, since you have to be very held in and that may not work as well. Halters are another no-no. A dress with a dropped waist helps when balanced with a full skirt.

Small bust: The best type of gown for a small bust has a neckline with some kind of detail, such as draping or shirring at the neckline that will give the illusion of a larger bust. Wear on-the-shoulder necklines with intricate details and beadwork. The empire style, with a seam under the bust line, is also a good choice.

Broad shoulders: Strapless gowns are great for broad shoulders because they de-emphasize the broadness of the back. A halter style is even better. Select a dress with a narrow bodice that offsets your shoulders and helps create an hourglass shape. Avoid the off-the-shoulder look, as it only makes your broad shoulders look broader.

Narrow shoulders: Off-the-shoulder and shawl collars look the most flattering. Straps are a good option. Dresses with thicker straps make the shoulders look wider than skinny straps; wide-set straps would be better than those set more closely to the neck. Avoid halter tops and strapless styles, as they will only accentuate narrow shoulders.

Short neck: Wear strapless, or something with spaghetti straps or a V-neckline. Avoid collars of any kind, along with jewel and bateau necklines. Anything closed around the neck will only make it look shorter. If your whole neckline is opened up, it will bring the eye toward the bust area, away from the neck. Also consider wearing your hair pulled up to create space from the shoulders up.

While you cannot predict the outcome by arming yourself with a set of rules, your goal is to discover the right combination of neckline, waistline, and skirt style that come together to create the perfect gown for your day, one that flatters your body the most.

CHAPTER SIX

YOUR BRIDAL STYLE

WEDDING DRESS SILHOUETTES

The walk down the aisle is the moment of a lifetime—a moment to be treasured forever.

As the center of attention, every bride dreams of being the picture of style, elegance, and beauty on her special day, and selecting the right gown can help make that dream come true. It is that magical garment you envisioned wearing on your most important day, the one that plays up your best features and represents your style and personality.

On your journey to finding this masterpiece, the wedding dress of your dreams, it will help if you familiarize yourself with the terminology as well as the basic bridal silhouettes available to you.

With the overwhelming number of choices flooding the bridal marketplace, bear in mind that bridal salons generally stock a mixture of different silhouettes in their collection in order to cater to brides of different figures and tastes.

There are many features that go into the design of a bridal gown. A dress is distinguished not only by its fundamental shape, but also by its fabric; decorative details, such as tucks, pleats, ruffles, and flounces; and embellishments like lace and embroidery. Various cuts of sleeves and necklines work with nearly every style to make a dress unique.

The terminology in this chapter will help you create the basis for the style you are searching for.

Determining the silhouette you would like to try on would be the first step in shopping for your bridal dress. In Chapter 5: Lines That Flatter: *Choosing a Style for Your Figure,* we looked at your body type and determined which dress styles are best for your body shape, ones that would be most flattering on you. That list is a good place to take with you when you start shopping for your gown.

BRIDAL SILHOUETTES

A-line: Universally wearable, the A-line has a fitted torso, with the skirt falling in a slightly flared, triangular shape (hence, the "A" line). The A-line is versatile; it may or may not have a seam at the waist, which may be higher or lower than the natural waistline, and the close-fitting bodice may be strapless or have any type of neckline. Flattering to all figures, this style is ideal for short brides seeking a longer line and is an especially smart option for larger and full-figured women because it is the most forgiving silhouette and an elegant alternative for anyone who wants to camouflage below-the-waist issues.

Recommended for all body types.

Ball Gown: Introduced by Queen Victoria, this style is never out of fashion. This is considered the most romantic of all bridal silhouettes. It features a fitted top, a small waist (natural or dropped), and a voluminous skirt with petticoats. Most flattering on women of at least average height with hourglass or full figures, this style's full skirt will overwhelm a petite, and even a particularly buxom, bride.

Depending on the fabric and embellishments, the skirt can appear weightless or heavy.

This is a popular style for brides having big weddings, as it has a very regal look.

Column/Sheath: Popularized in the 1950s by Marilyn Monroe, this body-hugging profile is artfully crafted with darts, tucks, and seams. The narrow, form-fitting style is devoid of any demarcation, as the silhouette falls directly from the neckline to the hem with no attaching seams. Some sheaths are cut on a bias, causing them to cling to the body. There is no doubt that this kind of body-conscious dress demands a lot from the wearer. If you're built for a bikini, go for it: You couldn't present the world a more enticing view from the altar. A great choice for a tall, slim-hipped woman, and equally becoming on a petite, slender bride. The effect will differ depending on the weight and drape of the fabric.

Avoid this style if you have narrow shoulders and wide hips.

Empire: This neoclassical style of dress was popularized after the French Revolution by Napoleon's wife Josephine. The very high waist and sheer materials she chose caused a sensation. It quickly became one of the most popular and regal looks shown on the runway. The empire dress has a raised waistline, starting just under the bust, attached to a flowing skirt that may be straight, slightly flared, or even as wide as an A-line.

It flatters the small-breasted woman, and because of the long lines created by the raised waist, it is ideal for a petite bride.

Mermaid/Fit and Flare: A narrow style where the bodice is elongated to attach with a skirt that flares from below the lower hips or just below the knee.

Great for a woman with a curvaceous body and an hourglass figure, this style shows off a whittled waistline while at the same time accentuating the bust and hips.

Princess: Closely related to the A-line, with a slender bodice and broad, ungathered skirt, this is a popular pick for both formal and informal weddings. The style has uninterrupted full-length vertical seams that begin at the neckline, skim the natural waist, and slide over the hip bones, with universally flattering and slimming effect. The seams may be piped, beaded or otherwise accentuated.

This is a perfect silhouette for tall, slim women who want a bit of a curve, as well as short-waisted women, as it lends an elongated effect.

Not recommended for thick waists, as it draws attention to the middle.

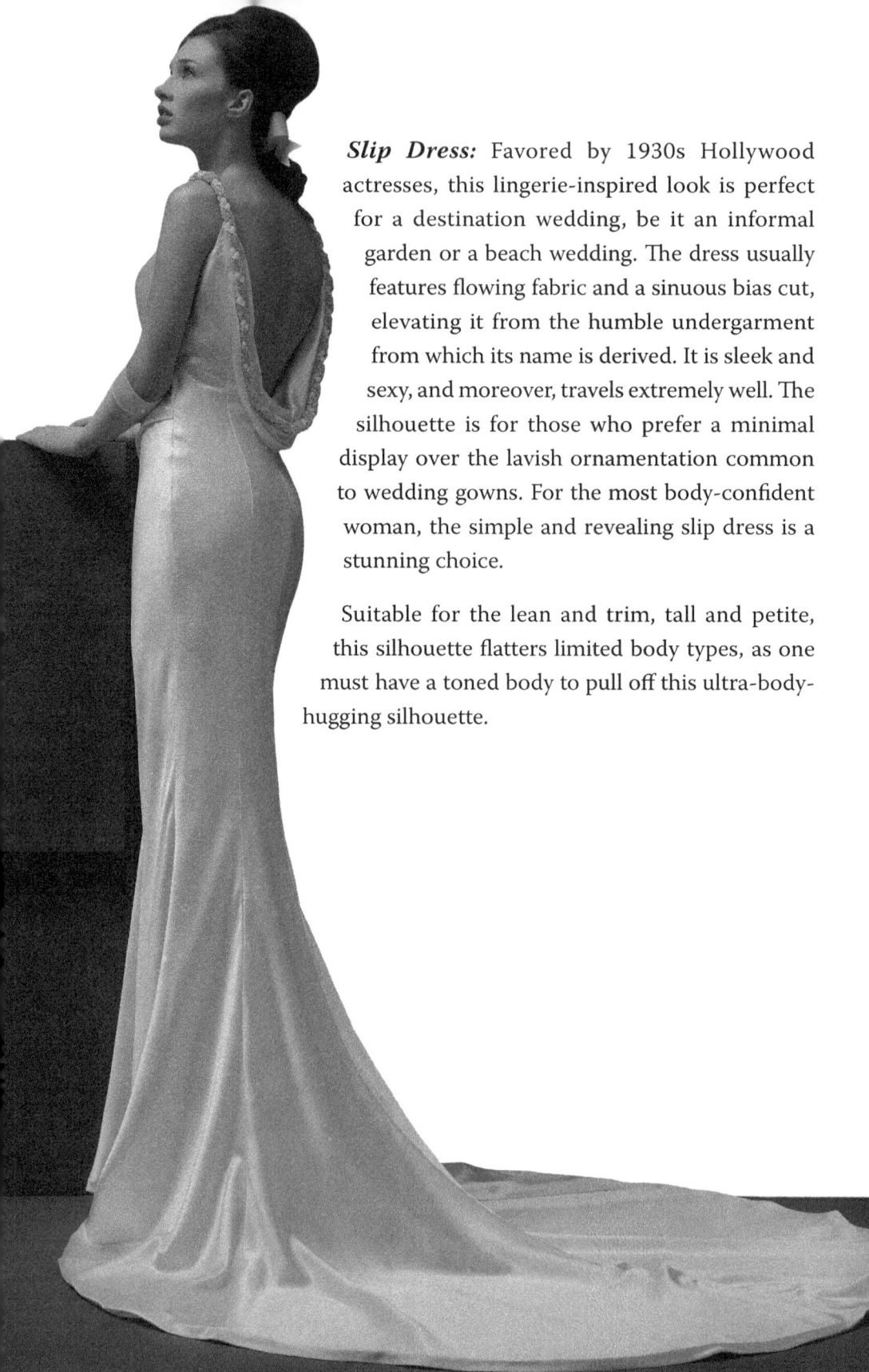

Slip Dress: Favored by 1930s Hollywood actresses, this lingerie-inspired look is perfect for a destination wedding, be it an informal garden or a beach wedding. The dress usually features flowing fabric and a sinuous bias cut, elevating it from the humble undergarment from which its name is derived. It is sleek and sexy, and moreover, travels extremely well. The silhouette is for those who prefer a minimal display over the lavish ornamentation common to wedding gowns. For the most body-confident woman, the simple and revealing slip dress is a stunning choice.

Suitable for the lean and trim, tall and petite, this silhouette flatters limited body types, as one must have a toned body to pull off this ultra-body-hugging silhouette.

THE BODICE

The bodice is the part of the dress that encompasses the entire torso and includes the bust, waist, and the hips. Finding the most flattering bodice style for your figure is key.

The Corset: A structured bodice, with a stiff inner layer of fabric, often supported by metal or plastic bands referred to as "stays" or "bones," which can be visible in some cases depending on the design, to create a smooth torso. Some corsets have lacing that snakes up the back, or the front.

About the corset . . .

When Phoebe married on Friends in my lilac St. Pucchi gown, the visible corset look that I had long ago introduced finally took off. Prior to that, bridal buyers could not wrap their minds around the idea that a bride would ever wish to wear such a controversial look. It was definitely not a traditional "look" in bridal.

However, since the highly publicized scene on Friends, the corset has seen a revival in contemporary high bridal fashion, and has transitioned from an item of underwear to outerwear. During the 1990s, the corset look became an integral part of my work, and I designed many ultra-feminine, fashionable, and couture corset bodices in materials as varied as duchess satin, silk Dupioni, and crushed silk taffeta. Some have been artfully embroidered with crystals and pearls, while others have been all about the lines and curves of the boning.

Regarded as the most essential garment worn during the Renaissance period, it also received the bad rap of being an instrument of torture and ill health. We know now that much of what we heard or read about was false and exaggerated. In reality, the corset was a symbol of social status and self-discipline as well as beauty and youthful allure. By the sixteenth century, corsets were primarily worn by aristocratic women and girls in order to attain a slender waist and an erect posture. There was much prestige associated with corsetry.

Do corsets contribute to comfort? Fashion before ease is the motto here! Sacrifice for a fantastic form is the key. Some things corsets do offer are a cinched waist, flattened abdomen, and lifted breasts.

There are as many types of corsets as there are bodices and necklines. Remember the scene in Gone With the Wind *when Scarlett O'Hara was laced into her corset? Or the costumes in* Dangerous Liaisons? *Most women wore some sort of body-shaping foundation garment throughout the 1950s and 1960s. But in modern times, diet and physical exercise as well as liposuction, plastic surgery, and "body sculpting" have contributed to a shift in attitudes toward the bodice, and the corset has not had such an important role.*

Fashion's focus on the waist is definitely not a passing trend. Corsetry is a form of body modification that has an important impact on women's lives.

Laced bodices resembling a corset are closed corsets that are laced up on the center back. The corset lace starts either at the bottom or at the top and is zigzagged through the staggered holes on each side in a series of crossings. We have also created double corset ties, where one starts from the top and another from the bottom and both meet and tie in the middle. Sometimes the vertically set bones are visible all around, but in most cases, the pockets with inserted bones/metal are built underneath the outer shell so as not to be visible. Open corsets are either laced up at the center front or fastened at the center front with a number of hooks and eyes, sometimes with as much as eighteen to twenty-four pairs.

A corset can be either fully boned or half-boned, depending on the style, with as much rigidity as the support the design calls for. Whalebone bodices with a different number of bones or stays are added around the sides of the corset. The direction of the bones is also important, as they help to shape the figure and narrow the waist.

Many brides tend to wear boned corsets or "stays," also called girdles or long-line bras, as the foundation garment under their bridal gown since it is easier to fit the dress over a firm foundation, and it also contributes to an erect posture. For brides wearing figure-hugging slim silhouettes, the right form-fitting all-in-one foundation that offers smooth, supple control from the bust through the thighs can make all the difference for a smooth fit into sheath dresses.

Empire: A style where the waistline begins just below the bust, usually having a low-cut front neckline and distinctive back line.

Halter: The halter bodice is made of split panels attached at the front, either under the bust or at the natural waist, and is connected with a clasp at the nape of the neck.

One-shoulder: One arm is demurely dressed, and the other bare.

Tank: A sleeveless bodice resembling a tank top.

NECKLINES AND BACKLINES

The neckline is the most important and powerful feature of a wedding gown. The three most important elements to consider when choosing the neckline are body type, bust size, and face shape.

Body type: Slender women of average size can carry off most necklines. However, those on the heavier side should opt for necklines that can elongate and make them look slimmer, such as square or

V-necklines. For extremely thin women, the bateau, scoop, and jewel necklines, with their curves and width, will help give a more rounded appearance to the face.

Shoulder width is also a factor when choosing the most flattering neckline. Necklines like the scoop and V help shift the focus from large shoulders, while the bateau and lower-cut necklines that stretch horizontally are more flattering on those with very narrow shoulders.

Bust size: The size of your bust plays a large role in what neckline will look best on you. Of all the necklines, the illusion neckline is the one that is universally flattering on most brides. Brides with moderate or average busts look good in almost any neckline. High necklines like the Queen Anne, bateau, and sweetheart create the illusion of curves and add volume to the chest and are most flattering on small-chested brides. Brides with large busts should avoid the plunging, deep V, and sweetheart necklines, and opt instead for supportive necklines like the scoop, Queen Anne, or V-necklines instead.

Face shape: The shape of your face plays a role in the neckline most suited to you. Oval faces look good in almost any neckline. Brides with long, narrow faces look best in horizontal necklines such as the bateau and off-the-shoulder, while those with round faces should look for V, square, or jewel necklines instead of a wider neckline, which may add further fullness to your face. Square and heart-shaped faces look best in scoop, V, bateau, or jewel necklines.

Bear in mind, though, that this is only a guideline, and there are several variations for each neckline. It is possible that a certain variation may work quite well for you. Your bridal consultant will be able to guide you to find one most flattering neckline.

FRONT NECKLINES

Bateau: Also known as the Sabrina neckline. Wide-necked and shaped like a boat, it follows a line curving slightly below the collarbone. Boosts bust. Calls attention to your shoulders for a face-widening effect.

> *Good for:* If you are flat-chested or have an oval or heart-shaped face.
>
> *Not so good for:* Busty brides, those with square or round faces.

Square: Shaped like a half-square or rectangle with straps. The depth may vary from shallow to deep, and it can be either narrow or wide.

> *Good for:* Well-endowed busts (cuts low, but is not too revealing) and particularly those with round or heart-shaped faces.
>
> *Not so good for:* Almost no one.

Cowl: Features fabric that has a draped effect and loosely hangs around the neck of the dress.

> ***Good for:*** The medium-to-small-chested bride.
>
> ***Not so good for:*** Busty brides.

Halter: Straps wrap around the neck and close at the back to accentuate the shoulders. It is stylish and slimming and may be cut high to look very modest or cut low to reveal cleavage.

> ***Good for:*** Those with long and thin necks and great shoulders.
>
> ***Not so good for:*** Narrow or broad shoulders, those needing bra support, and women with thick, short necks.

Illusion: A transparent panel or yoke made of tulle, net, or lace, covering the area from the bust to the collar. Classic and ethereal, it offers support and gives the gown a modest, yet sophisticated look.

> ***Good for:*** Almost everyone.

Jewel: Similar to a T-shirt neckline, it encircles the base of the neck. It is modest and covers the upper torso, shoulders, and collarbones and is a perfect choice for formal wedding ceremonies.

> ***Good for:*** The flat-chested bride. It softens a square face, and is also great for those with round and heart-shaped faces.
>
> ***Not so good for:*** Busty brides and those with oval faces.

Off-the-shoulder: Below the shoulders with sleeves. Shows off collarbones, shoulders, and décolletage.

>***Good for:*** Well-endowed busts and slender brides with well-toned arms and a beautiful neck.
>
>***Not so good for:*** Broad, thick shoulders and thicker necks.

Portrait: Dramatic collar that envelopes the shoulders with a shawl effect, leaving them bare, usually with a low front neckline.

>***Good for:*** Great collarbones.
>
>***Not so good for:*** Undefined or bony collarbones.

Queen Anne: Higher up in the back and along the sides of the neck, curving down to a center front point, similar to a sweetheart dip. Somewhat formal, very elegant, and with a deep front can be very sexy.

>***Good for:*** Those with long, thin necks.
>
>***Not so good for:*** Short, thick necks.

Scoop: U-shaped, can be cut low. Also known as the ballerina neckline. Draws attention to the neck and face and is universally flattering.

>***Good for:*** Almost everyone, especially those with square, oval and heart-shaped faces.

Asymmetric: Stylish one-shoulder design, drapes toward just one shoulder, leaving the other one exposed, reminiscent of Greek goddesses. Great for beach and garden weddings.

> ***Good for:*** Great collarbones, long necks, narrow shoulders, and thin arms.
>
> ***Not so good for:*** The broad-shouldered.

Spaghetti straps: Thin straps supporting the bodice. The neckline may be scoop, V, or sweetheart. Straps can be adorned with jewels. Stylish, youthful, and fashionable.

> ***Good for:*** Those with well-toned shoulders and elegant collarbones.
>
> ***Not so good for:*** Thicker necks and shoulders.

Strapless: Cut straight across or with a notch or side peaks or slightly curved for a softer look. Bodice without straps or sleeves. Draws instant focus to the upper body.

> ***Good for:*** Those with moderate-size busts and broad or thick shoulders.
>
> ***Not so good for:*** Smaller chests (unless a push-up bra is worn) as well as tall and thin women, as it emphasizes their height and makes them look skinny.

Sweetheart: Resembles the upper half of a heart, closely following the natural curves of the bust, and dips in the center. Elegantly accentuates the neck, shoulders, and décolletage.

> ***Good for:*** Those with slender arms and shoulders.
>
> ***Not so good for:*** Large-chested brides.

V-neckline: Dips down into a V in the center front. Elongates the neck and de-emphasizes the bust. Can be deep-cut and plunging for a sexy look, or higher for a modest and elegant look.

> ***Good for:*** B and C cups and especially those with round, square, and oval faces.
>
> ***Not so good for:*** A or D cups (body will seem too empty or too full), and those with a heart-shaped face.

Wedding band collar: A high-band collar like a mock turtleneck, fits closely around the neck.

> ***Good for:*** Those with long, slim necks, and round as well as oval faces.
>
> ***Not so good for:*** Short, thick necks and square or heart-shaped faces.

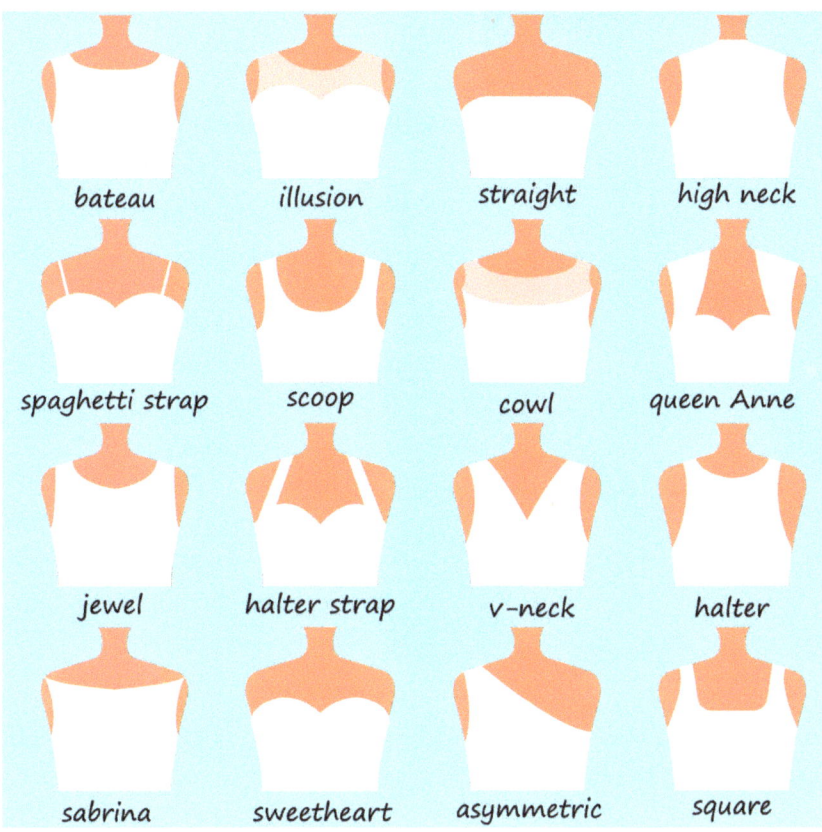

BACK NECKLINES

The back line is extremely important, as it enhances the area from the nape of the neck to the arch of the back. The back provides a blank canvas and can contribute to the sexiness as well as an ultra-stylish look of the dress.

Backless: A barely there back where the gown exposes the broad expanse of the back, in the case of halter dresses.

Illusion: A sheer, translucent fabric, such as net, tulle, or lace, covering an exposed area of the back.

Keyhole: A circular, oval, or tear-shaped opening to expose a section of the back.

Scoop: A low, rounded backline dipping from the shoulders in a half-circle or oval shape.

Surplice: Two panels that overlap one another and attach or tie at the waist.

V-line: Dips down into a V in the center back.

WAISTLINES

Now it is time to determine what kind of waistline you would like to wear. The waistline of your wedding dress is one of the key elements in defining your look. It can make you look tall or short, slender or curvy, and help balance your overall look.

Please note, however, that a dress may drape differently on different body types, and the best way to see is to try them on and determine for yourself what you feel best in.

Below are the various options:

Asymmetrical: Seam angles down to one side, draping the body asymmetrically, usually in a diagonal fashion.

Good for: Hourglass figures and those who are tall and slim.

Not so great for: Apple shapes, those with larger waistlines, and shorter brides.

Basque waist: Slightly elongated V-shape with the point dipping as much as three to five inches at the center front. Usually found on structured ball gowns, this waistline helps minimize the hips while creating an illusion of length. Helps elongate the torso; the tapering helps trim a thick middle.

> *Good for:* Pear-shaped and hourglass figures, and those who are short-waisted.
>
> *Not so great for:* Apple-shaped figures, and those with a larger waistline.

Curved Basque: Similar to Basque, though rounded at the center front.

Blouson: Fabric is gathered just at or below the waist, creating a soft fullness.

Dropped waist: Falls to several inches below the natural waistline, straight across. Creates an illusion of a longer, leaner torso.

> *Good for:* Hourglass figures, and those with a small natural waistline or wide hips.
>
> *Not so great for:* Petite brides or those with an already low natural waistline.

Empire: A high waist that starts just below the bust. Draws attention to the chest.

> *Good for:* Shorter brides who wish to look lean, and tall brides with small busts.
>
> *Not so great for:* Large-chested women.

Inverted Basque: Slightly elongated, rising to a point at the center front.

> *Good for:* Pear-shaped and hourglass figures.
>
> *Not so great for:* Apple-shaped figures, and those with a larger waistline.

Natural waist: Waist seam of dress coincides with the actual waistline, just above the hips.

> *Good for:* Hourglass figures, and those with a slender waist. On a ballgown, it looks good on pear-shaped figures as well.
>
> *Not so great for:* Apple-shaped figures.

SLEEVES

Sleeves add a classic element to the wedding dress. However, long sleeves in general have their limitations unless they are cut on the bias and made of stretch fabrics, as you may not be able to raise your arms higher than your shoulders. Still, they add a romantic feel to the bridal gown.

Ball gown/Pouf: Short, full, gathered sleeves worn on or off the shoulders.

Balloon: Voluminous sleeves puffing out from the shoulder, either short or long.

Bell: Narrow at the top, flaring at the bottom in a bell shape.

Bishop: Lightly gathered at the shoulders and full to the elbow, then fitted at the cuff.

Cap: Very short, fitted sleeves with no shoulder seam, that just cover the shoulder. Gives less coverage than short sleeves.

Dolman: Very wide at the armhole, extending to a tight cuff at either the elbow or wrist.

Elbow-length: Varying styles ending at the elbow.

Gauntlet: Detachable lace or fabric sleeves that cover the forearm to the wrist.

Juliet: Long sleeves, with a pouf at the top, then long and straight.

Long, fitted: A long sleeve with little or no fullness that ends either in a straight line at wrist, or falls to a point over the top of the hand (fitted point).

Poet: Fitted and narrower at the top, ending in wide ruffles or pleats.

Renaissance/Leg o' mutton: Long sleeves that are full and rounded from the shoulder to just above the elbow, tapering to a fitted sleeve to the wrist.

Short, fitted: Short, fitted sleeves worn on the shoulder.

Short, tunnel: Short, off-the-shoulder sleeve (sometimes shirred).

Three-quarter-length: Ends between the elbow and wrist.

Tulip: Set-in sleeves that overlap to create a tulip effect.

SKIRT DETAILS

Box pleats: A pleat where the fabric is folded at two points and wrapped under the fold, creating a box-like effect.

Bustle: A gathering of fabric at the back of the waistline, in several interims going all the way down the train.

Flounce: A wide piece of fabric or lace gathered and attached at the hem. Often this fabric is cut on the bias to give it movement.

Handkerchief hem: Cut like square handkerchief panels and placed all around the hem.

Pannier: Gathered fabric over the sides of the hips.

Peplum: A short overskirt or flounce attached at the waist.

Redingote: Skirt panels open from the waist seam, along the entire front to reveal a dress or petticoat worn underneath.

Tiered: Layered panels of fabric that fall from the waist to the hem in varying lengths.

SKIRT LENGTHS

Depending on the type of ceremony, such as formal or informal, different skirt lengths must be considered. Formal ceremonies generally call for a floor-length dress, while informal ceremonies make exceptions for varying lengths.

Asymmetrical: Hemline is longer on one side than the other.

Ballet/Ballerina: Hemline falls to just above the ankles, generally 4 to 6 inches from the floor

Floor-length: Hemline falls a half-inch to two inches from the floor.

Intermission-length/High-low: Hemline falls slightly below or midway between the knee and ankle in front, graduating to floor-length in back.

Mini: Hemline falls several inches above the knee.

Street-length: Hemline falls to just about, or slightly below, the knee.

Tea-length: Hemline falls to the lower part of the calf, generally eight to ten inches from the floor.

Tulip: Lower part of the skirt overlaps to create a tulip effect.

TRAIN BASICS

How important is the train on a wedding dress? Should your dress have a train? If so, what train length is appropriate?

You can either forgo the train entirely or decide on the train length based on your venue and the type of wedding you plan on having. Wedding trains are undoubtedly classic and an important factor that sets a bridal dress apart from any other. Ideal train lengths also depend on how formal the function is and your comfort level.

Trains come in various lengths and widths, and there is even an option to have a detachable train that can be removed after the ceremony to allow ease of movement during the reception and to dance unencumbered.

Here are some train options to consider:

Cathedral: This is a formal train that extends approximately three yards from the back of the waist, and approximately twenty-four to twenty-eight inches on the floor. It is majestic in appearance and ideal for a traditional church ceremony or a formal wedding. The cathedral train needs to be bustled after the ceremony.

Chapel: The chapel train is shorter than a cathedral train, although just as dramatic, and is probably the most common style of train, since it does not require a lot of maintenance but still gives off a striking look during the ceremony. It extends approximately one and a half yards from the back of the waist, and no more than fifteen to twenty inches on the floor. Suitable for formal and semi-formal weddings.

Court: The court train is shorter in length than the chapel train, but longer than a sweep train. It extends approximately one yard from the back waist and can be easily managed without a lot of fuss. Suitable for both formal and semi-formal ceremonies.

Sweep: This is the shortest train, sweeping a few inches out but not enough to bustle. It is stylish and the best one to wear at an outdoor wedding, where it would be impossible to have a long train as it would catch whatever is on the ground.

Trumpet/Fishtail: Ultra-slender and popular on the red carpet, this train slithers eight to twelve inches behind a form-fitting and slinky gown.

Floor-length: This train is almost non-existent, barely falling a half to one and a half inches from the floor. It is a great one to wear at an outdoor wedding—beach or garden—and balances style and simplicity.

Monarch/Royal cathedral: This is the longest and most dramatic train length, extending approximately four or more yards from the waist. It needs a more complex bustle because of its width and length and will usually require assistance when walking down the aisle.

Semi-cathedral: Falls between the Chapel and Cathedral length and extends approximately two yards from the waistline.

Watteau: A train made of a single panel of long fabric that attaches to the back of the gown, typically at or just below the shoulders and falling to the hemline.

Some venues may make a train more difficult to manage, such as outdoor weddings at the beach or in nature. Therefore, consider the venue—a black-tie ceremony or a casual affair, indoors or outdoors—as well as your activities for the day before making your final decision on what length of train to go for. And if the longer train is your preference, then consider having it bustled (see Chapter 15: All About the Bustle). Your bridal consultant can suggest which type of bustle would look best.

With so many choices, and such a delightful confusion of silhouettes and styles, what calls out the most to you?

Chapter Seven

FABRICS, LACES, AND TRIMS

Satin, tulle, and Shantung have you in a whirl?

Have you ever been confused about the difference between fabrics?

And what about different finishes?

To be clear, a fabric is the name of the actual type of thread used to create the material, and a finish is the description of what the fabric looks and feels like after it is woven.

The beauty of a wedding dress very much depends on the fabric it is created from. The entire effect and feel of a dress can be transformed simply by varying the fabric used. This is because the fabric determines how a dress drapes and whether it is suitable for the venue and the season of your wedding day.

Knowing, then, the importance of the role fabric plays in the construction of your gown, it would help to have a basic knowledge to help you better choose the style you would like to wear.

FABRICS

One important fact to note when choosing fabrics is that most can be made of pure silk, silk blends, or polyester, the most expensive fabrics being made of pure (100 percent) silk.

Batiste: A fine cloth made from cotton, wool, polyester, or a blend, and the softest of the lightweight opaque fabrics.

Bengaline: A woven fabric with a rib effect that is often embossed with a floral or moiré pattern.

Brocade: A unique woven pattern, often employing threads of more than one color to depict a raised design against a flat background. It has a finish similar to damask, but heavier.

Charmeuse: A luxury fabric made from silk with a soft satin finish. Today, the definition of charmeuse fabric has expanded to incorporate a less-expensive polyester version. Charmeuse has a floating appearance that drapes very well, especially for bridal and formal wear. It has a lightweight finish, similar to satin but softer. The fabric typically works well with a more body-conscious, bias-cut silhouette.

Chiffon: A lightweight, balanced plain-woven sheer fabric with a soft finish, usually made from silk, silk blends, or rayon yarns. It has some stretch and a slightly rough feel. Under a magnifying glass, it resembles a fine net or mesh, which gives chiffon some see-through properties. Silk chiffon can be dyed to almost any shade, but chiffon made from polyester can be difficult to dye. Chiffon drapes well and is a good choice for spring and summer weddings.

Crêpe: A light silk, wool, or synthetic fiber fabric with a distinctively soft and crisp, crinkled appearance. It is most typically used for dresses that feature draping and those that are form-fitting, as it flows elegantly and softly hugs the body.

Damask: Classical damask is made from silk, although the term is now widely used to refer to the style of weaving, regardless of the material used. Damask is characterized by a background of lustrous fabric against which raised designs appear, similar to brocade but on a lighter fabric. It is a type of textile historically used to make jackets and other heavy outer garments.

Duchess satin: Also known as silk-faced satin, it is an elegant and lustrous fabric, shiny, heavy, and luxurious. Often used for couture wedding gowns, it has been around since the latter part of the Middle Ages, originating in ancient China. Duchess satin has a soft texture with a lot of body and sheen, and is a popular choice for wedding gowns because it drapes well, helping to create full and beautiful skirts. Duchess satin is usually made from silk fibers, although it can also contain polyester, rayon, or acetate filler. Designers prefer this material because the skirt keeps its full curves, instead of fluttering, as would a thinner fabric.

Dupioni (also referred to as Douppioni or Dupion): A plain-weave, crisp type of silk fabric, produced by using fine thread in the warp and uneven thread reeled from two or more entangled cocoons in the weft. This creates tightly-woven yardage with a highly lustrous surface. The finish is similar to Shantung but with thicker, coarser fibers and a slight sheen.

English net: Soft, pliable netting made with fine cotton yarn, ideal for special occasion dresses, accessories, bridal veiling, and trim. Softer than tulle, more sheer than chiffon, and with a weight and richness that creates a lovely, light drape.

Faille: Usually quite heavy, faille is a plain weave fabric with pronounced, fairly flat crosswise ribs and a silky, somewhat lustrous surface. Silk faille is a flat-ribbed fabric with a light silken luster. This faille has excellent drape and is beautiful in suits, jackets, and dresses.

Gazar (also gazaar): A silk or organza plain weave fabric made with high-twist double yarns woven as one. Gazar has a crisp hand and a smooth texture. Silk gazar is much used in bridal and evening fashion due to its ability to hold its shape.

Georgette: A sheer, lightweight, dull-finished crêpe fabric named after the early twentieth-century French dressmaker Georgette de la Plante. Typically, georgette fabric is made from silk, but occasionally it is also made from other materials such as rayon and polyester. It's very lightweight and a good choice for warm weather.

Illusion: A very fine, sheer net fabric usually made of nylon or silk. Used for veils and overlays on skirts. It can be light as air or more sturdy, depending on the weave, and has a cobweb appearance.

Jacquard: A raised design or pattern woven into a fabric (usually satin), as opposed to being printed on the fabric. Jacquard weaves have a varying drape ability and durability depending on which fibers are used.

Lamé: A lightweight fabric woven or knit with metallic yarns.

Linen: Made from flax, this fabric has a beautiful, natural texture but is prone to wrinkles.

Organdy (also organdie): The sheerest and crispest cotton cloth made. Combed yarns contribute to its appearance. Because of its stiffness and fiber content, it is very prone to wrinkling. Organdy is popularly used in overlays and embellishments and is stiff enough to give structure to the gown.

Organza: A thin, sheer fabric traditionally made from silk, with a crystal-like surface. Many modern organza fabrics are woven with synthetic filament fibers such as polyester or nylon. The fabric is soft enough for a wedding gown and is also used as overlays and embellishments.

Ottoman: A heavy, stiff fabric with larger ribs than faille, with a pronounced ribbed or corded effect, often made of silk or a mixture of cotton and other silk-like yarns. Ottoman made of pure silk is very expensive, so artificial silk is used instead to create a more affordable alternative.

Peau-de-Soie: Also known as de-lusted satin, this is a soft, satin-faced, good-quality cloth of silk or rayon that has a dull luster and grainy appearance with very fine ribs. It is used to make bridal dresses, coats, trimmings, etc.

Piqué: Piqué, or marcella, refers to a weaving style. A piqué fabric is a knit or woven fabric with patterns of fine ribbing or cording created with a dobby loom attachment. Piqué fabrics are medium-weight and usually made with cotton fiber. The fabric wrinkles badly unless given a wrinkle-free finish.

Point d'esprit: Sometimes classified as a type of lace, it is actually a fine bobbinet or tulle with oval or square dots woven in an irregular pattern.

Polyester: An inexpensive, man-made fabric that can be made to look like a version of any other fabric. Polyester fabrics can provide specific advantages over natural fabrics, such as improved wrinkle resistance, durability, and high color retention.

Raw silk: Often confused with silk Dupioni, raw silk is quite difficult to find. It is a lot heavier than silk Dupioni, with a much thicker texture and many more "slubs," which are thick imperfections in a fiber. It is best used for suits and jackets and structured dresses or skirts. It is quite bulky and does not drape well and is not really suitable for wedding gowns.

Rayon: Initially called "imitation silk," rayon is similar to silk, but with a lighter hand and more drape, as well as more elasticity. It is a synthetic fabric made from plant fibers. Although affordable, it is easily damaged by water.

Satin: A weave that typically has a glossy surface and a dull back. A silk finish gives satin a smooth and tightly woven texture, with a glossy sheen on the face and a dull underside. Most satins are made with silk thread, but the fabric can also be made with other materials like polyester, acetate, nylon, and rayon. Some types, called double-faced satins, are made to be shiny on both sides by using two sets of warp strands. Satin is an ideal choice for a formal wedding and for cooler weather, although the heavy structure may not be as appropriate for an outdoor wedding.

Shantung: A type of silk fabric historically originating from the province of Shandong, China. It is similar to Dupioni, but is slightly thinner and less irregular. Shantung is often used for bridal gowns. It has a rough texture, with imperfections similar to raw silk.

About the difference . . .

Aside from the difference of origin ("Dupioni" being Italian, and "Shantung" being Chinese), there is one clue that differentiates the two fabrics. Silk Dupioni has much more prominent slubs and is the thicker of the two materials. It has an almost rustic look, but the incredible sheen and the vibrancy of colors makes it suitable for bridal gowns and prom dresses. However, it does not drape well. In contrast, silk Shantung has hardly any slubs, and while it has a fair amount of body and crispness, it is much thinner than Dupioni, and therefore is more suitable for the more delicate styles. The Shantung can appear flowing and is appropriate for designs that require draping and softness.

Silk: A soft, fine, and lustrous fabric synonymous with luxury, silk is the epitome of style and sophistication. Silk adds an elegant and formal touch to most wedding gowns. Pure (100 percent) silk is very expensive, but silk blends are more reasonable.

About silk...

Silk is a natural protein fiber, composed mainly of fibroin, and is produced by certain insect larvae to form cocoons. The best-known silk is obtained from the cocoons of the larvae of the mulberry silkworm. The shimmering appearance of silk is due to the triangular prism-like structure of the silk fiber, which allows silk cloth to refract incoming light at different angles, thus producing different colors. Silk fabric was first developed in ancient China in the Neolithic Yangshao culture (fourth millennium BC), but other silks such as Thai silk and Indian silk have gained increasing popularity. In Thailand, women traditionally weave silk on hand looms and pass the skill on to their daughters, as weaving is considered to be a sign of maturity and eligibility for marriage. Thai silk textiles often use complicated patterns in various colors and styles. Most regions of Thailand have their own typical silks. A single thread filament is too thin to use on its own, so women combine many threads to produce a thicker, usable fiber. They do this by hand-reeling the threads onto a wooden spindle to produce a uniform strand of raw silk. The process takes around forty hours to produce half of a kilogram of silk.

Silk Mikado: A brand of blended silk, usually heavier than 100 percent silk, Mikado is a wonderful choice for modern, architectural gowns. It is less shiny than satin, and less matte than crêpe, and wrinkles less than both fabrics. Mikado is frequently used for fall and winter wedding gowns.

Stretch illusion: A fine net made with Lycra yarn.

Taffeta: A crisp, smooth fabric, with a crosswise rib and a slight sheen. The fabric is historically made from silk, but today can be made from many different fibers, including artificial fibers like nylon and rayon. Many people associate this fabric with luxury and high-end wedding gowns and evening dresses. It is often used in ball gowns and gowns that need structure. The fabric usually has a very tight weave, and the weave is plain. Taffeta is famous for being very stiff and crisp, generating rustling sounds when people move in it. Yarn-dyed fabric tends to be especially stiff, while piece-dyed garments are softer and more flexible. The fabric is also very soft and smooth to the touch, and it has a famously lustrous and shimmering appearance.

Thai silk: A super-fine, high-quality silk similar in weight and feel to Dupioni, but much smoother and crisper, and has almost no slubs. It is more expensive than Dupioni, with a superior quality, spectacular sheen, and vividness of color. Thai silk is best suited for structured gowns and big, full ballroom skirts, as well as A-line skirts and fitted bodices.

Tulle: A lightweight, very fine netting with a soft finish. It can be made of various fibers, including silk, nylon, and rayon. Tulle is most commonly used for veils and gowns and is often mixed with other fabrics. Tulle comes in a wide array of colors, and it can also easily be dyed to suit the needs of the consumer.

Tullonet: A coarse net with a stiff finish used to give fullness under skirts.

Twill: A type of textile weave with a pattern of diagonal parallel ribs (in contrast with a satin and plain weave). Silk twills are increasingly popular in couture bridal designs.

Voile: A soft, sheer fabric, usually made of 100 percent cotton or cotton blends including linen or polyester. The term comes from French, and means "veil." Because of its light weight, the fabric has the draping power of (although with more structure than) chiffon. Voile is ideal for sheaths and A-line skirts and designs that require a soft, casual look.

Velvet: A soft, thick fabric with a felted face and plain underside. It is a type of woven tufted fabric in which the cut threads are evenly distributed with a short, dense pile, giving it a distinctive feel. Velvet can be made from either synthetic or natural fibers.

LACES

Like snowflakes, no two laces are alike. Lace has been used in bridal wear from time immemorial. Lace and weddings is indeed a match made in heaven.

Even though some bodices and skirts are entirely overlaid with lace, more often than not, lace is used to accent certain parts of the bodice, sleeves, and hems. Apart from wedding dresses, lace is also an important element in veils, bolero jackets, wedding garters, and as trims for the bridal bouquet and handkerchiefs.

Different lace details determine whether it renders a modern or antique look to a wedding dress. Traditionally lace was handmade and hence more expensive, although much of the lace available today is machine-woven and more affordable.

From romantic and ethereal, from wispy forms to crisp, laser-cut details, the charm of lace continues to impress the bridal world while adding a whimsical, feminine, and romantic feel to the wedding gown.

Here is a glossary of the most popular laces used in bridal:

Alençon: Known as the queen of lace, this was the most pricey and coveted lace in the world. Originally produced by hand in Alençon, a town in Normandy, France, it is a light, airy needle lace made of linen thread. The lace starts as a sheer net background on which delicate floral and swirl designs are created by needlepoint and edged with heavy cotton or linen corded thread. Over time machines, took over, and Alençon lace has now been interpreted into more commercial versions. It is most popular among bridal designers.

Battenburg: Also known as "crochet" lace, the Battenburg lace was developed in the late 1800s and named after Queen Victoria's son-in-law. The lace gets its distinctive look by combining machine-woven tapes with hand stitching. It is a heavy lace made with patterns of linen braid and tape connected with decorative linen stitching. Battenburg lace remains a popular embellishment for women's clothing and wedding gowns.

Brocade: This type of lace is woven on shuttle looms and has rich woven and raised patterns, giving it a thicker feel unlike the delicate Chantilly lace. Metallic silver and gold threads add to its grandeur. Many brocade laces also use colored silk threads instead of the traditional white.

Chantilly: An extremely delicate needlepoint lace originating from the city of Chantilly in France. The lace has a fine mesh background on which delicate floral and scrolled designs are woven into a fine hexagonal mesh and with a soft, sweet, scalloped edge. Vintage Chantilly lace is expensive and in high demand, making it one of the most coveted laces in the bridal marketplace.

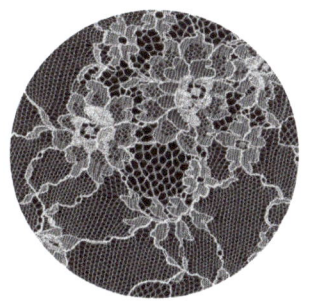

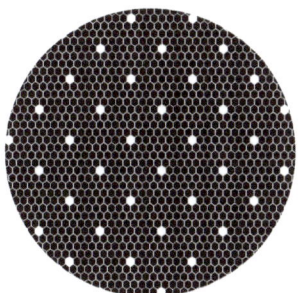

Dotted Swiss: Repeated small, regular circles over a net background.

Embroidered: There is a pronounced three-dimensional effect on this type of lace, with motifs that resemble embroidery on a base material ranging from illusion netting to thicker satins. Embroidered lace can be either hand-embroidered (more expensive) or machine-embroidered.

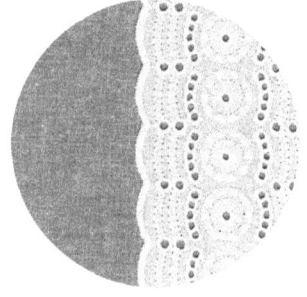

Eyelet: One of the most common laces, usually made of cotton. This casual lace is distinguished by the large holes or eyelets integrated into the pattern at regular intervals. It can be found in all shapes, sizes, and colors with a fundamental pattern, which is able to repeat infinitely. Common motifs are geometric shapes like diamonds, squares, and circles; floral themes; and simple abstract patterns. This type of lace looks best on dresses made for beach and garden weddings.

Guipure: Also known as Venetian lace, this is another type of French bobbin lace, but unlike the Chantilly lace, it is heavy and has an almost geometric look, with a large, repetitive pattern. It is created without a net background, instead using built-up layers of thread to create a textural, three-dimensional pattern. Guipure is a malleable lace that can be used well on the bodice, skirt, or train of any silhouette dress and is favored by many designers for its distinct characteristics.

Lyons: This is much like Chantilly lace. It has a floral design, and is made on a very finely woven hexagonal mesh. However, it's stiffer than the more delicate Chantilly, and the pattern is outlined with fine silk or cotton threads.

Schiffli: Also known as chemical lace, Schiffli lace is a form of machine-made lace. This method of lace-making is done by embroidering a pattern on a sacrificial fabric that has been chemically treated so as to disintegrate after the pattern has been created. This embroidery is typically done on a multi-head or multi-needle Schiffli machine or loom that has a very large, continuous, and overlapping embroidery field.  The lace pattern is designed so that the embroidery thread creates an interlocking series of threads that will, in essence, become a "stand-alone" piece of lace. After the embroidery is completed, the embroidered fabric is immersed in a solution that will not harm the embroidery thread but completely dissolves the sacrificial fabric, leaving just the lace.

Soutache: Often called Russian Braid or passementerie, a soutache is a narrow, flat, ornamental braid used to trim garments. In bridal, it is used to give a corded effect when twisted into scroll or floral designs on the fabrics, for a heavier dimensional effect.

Venise: Venise lace, or Point de Venise, is a needle lace that was first made in Italy in the seventeenth century. It is a machine-made imitation of Venetian needlepoint made by the burnt-out process and generally created on cotton. Unlike other laces, it is without a solid attached background, making it appear cut-out. Venise edging lace is stunning as wedding gown lace trim, and its dramatic weight and design makes it ideal for theatrical and dance costumes.

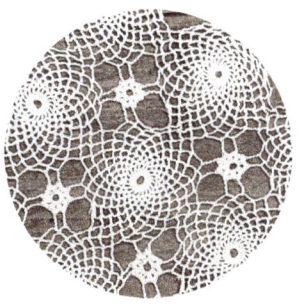

EMBROIDERY

Everyone who is familiar with St. Pucchi knows that from my very first bridal collection in 1985, each dress was hand-embroidered and hand-beaded. Personally, I believe in the magic of embroidery. Not only because it lends a unique look to your dress, but because the exquisite craftsmanship that goes into each creation makes a wedding gown bloom in a way that no lace can.

The art of embroidery dates back thousands of years, even before lace and woven cloths. Skilled artisans work on fine fabric that is stretched across a frame, called an embroidery hoop, one perfect stitch at a time.

At the St. Pucchi factory, as many as fifteen people spend several weeks on a single dress the old-fashioned way. Different kinds of threads, either cotton or silk, are used in various shades of white, ivory, blush, and champagne. Often, after the embroidery is done, it is repeated over to enhance the pattern with fancy threadwork in silver or gold, adding texture and romance to the luxurious fabric. Sometimes ribbon or cording is used instead or in conjunction with the above to create dimension, making the results more pronounced.

The embroidery process gives a designer free rein on where the pattern will be drawn and can range from tiny leaves and border accents to full-skirt masterpieces. It also allows one to mix contrasting threads and mix colors, which is somewhat limited when using ready-made laces.

The value of any dress is dependent on the intricacy and labor-intensiveness of the work that goes into it, as well as the amount of time it will take for the dress to be ready. Therefore, when making a decision, do make sure your choice meets the budget you have allocated to your dress.

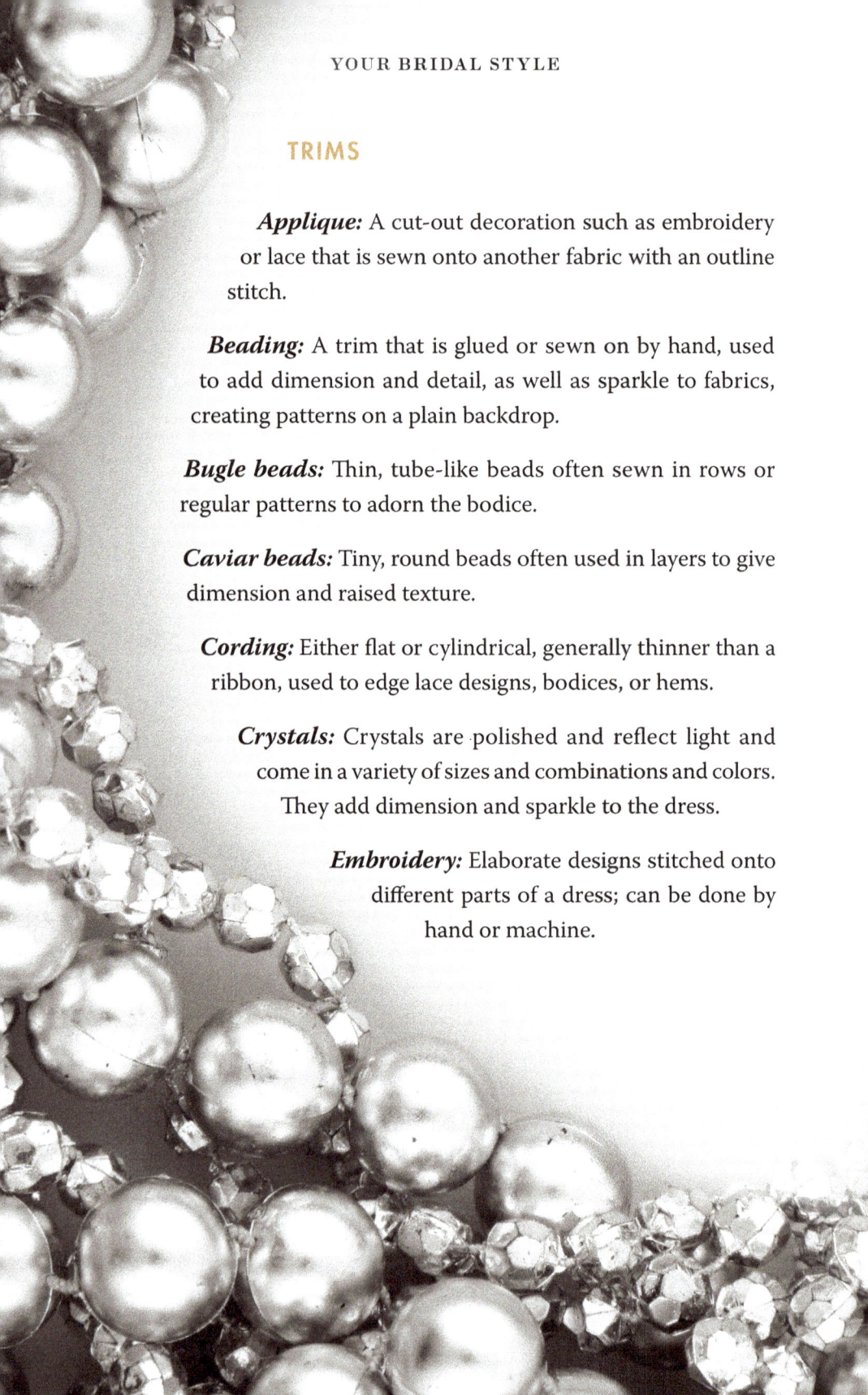

YOUR BRIDAL STYLE

TRIMS

Applique: A cut-out decoration such as embroidery or lace that is sewn onto another fabric with an outline stitch.

Beading: A trim that is glued or sewn on by hand, used to add dimension and detail, as well as sparkle to fabrics, creating patterns on a plain backdrop.

Bugle beads: Thin, tube-like beads often sewn in rows or regular patterns to adorn the bodice.

Caviar beads: Tiny, round beads often used in layers to give dimension and raised texture.

Cording: Either flat or cylindrical, generally thinner than a ribbon, used to edge lace designs, bodices, or hems.

Crystals: Crystals are polished and reflect light and come in a variety of sizes and combinations and colors. They add dimension and sparkle to the dress.

Embroidery: Elaborate designs stitched onto different parts of a dress; can be done by hand or machine.

Gems/Rhinestones: Imitation crystals, usually used instead of crystals to ornament soft gauzy fabrics on bodices, skirts, and veils.

Pailettes: Large and round or rectangular (similar to sequins), these come in distinctive shapes, designed to be anchored at one single point, leaving the rest to hang free, thus giving movement.

Sequins: Small, round reflective disks used in ornamentation, generally scattered to add sparkle and dimension to laces and fabrics.

Seed pearls: Small freshwater pearl beads in very small sizes—four millimeters or smaller.

Soutache: A narrow, flat, ornamental braid used to trim garments.

Personal style is all about details. Like juxtaposing traditional or edgy-chic dresses with pretty and glamorous accents, together they add up to a big statement.

CHAPTER EIGHT

COMMONLY USED TERMS EVERY BRIDE SHOULD KNOW BEFORE DRESS SHOPPING

Let's face it. Wedding dress shopping is not just another trip to a department store where you can pick a dress and take it home.

Shopping for a wedding dress is a full-on endeavor, an expedition, and a mission that will stay in your memory long after the day is over. So, it's a good idea to be well equipped and get your facts straight before you begin the search. For example, what is the difference between Guipure lace and Alençon lace? How about a bustle and a modesty piece?

Aside from obvious silhouettes such as A-line, sheath, column, ballgown—some details can make any bride seriously confused and frustrated. If you would like to be well-versed, and have some answers at your fingertips, here are ten most commonly used terms to know ahead of your biggest shopping trip.

1. ***Alençon lace:*** Originally produced by hand in Alençon, a town in Normandy, France, it is a light, airy needle lace made of linen thread. This is one of the most popular and traditional laces used on wedding dresses.

2. ***Boning:*** Plastic or metal sewn into the bodice of the dress, especially a corset on a strapless wedding gown, to ensure the fit is snug and the fabric does not droop.

3. ***Bustle:*** The art of pinning a train and securing it by using hidden hooks on the back of the dress so it does not drag around on the ground after the ceremony. There are several different ways to bustle. The French bustle is the most popular, whereby the train is tucked underneath and pinned or hooked to the fabric of the dress.

4. ***Chantilly lace:*** Delicate lace that originates from the city of Chantilly in France. This is one of the more popular laces used on wedding dresses. It comes in small, detailed patterns and look best when worn sheer over the arms, back, and neckline.

5. ***Court:*** Refers to a type of train that is short—generally three feet from the waist—and drags a few inches on the ground.

6. ***Crêpe:*** Thin, soft fabric with a slightly wrinkled surface, ideally used on a draped wedding gown or one that is form-fitting and clings to the body. Great for a beach wedding.

7. ***Dropped waist:*** A longer bodice attached to the skirt at the seam that falls below the natural waistline. Gives an illusion of a longer torso and looks best on taller women.

8. *Guipure lace:* French bobbin lace, used on the bodice, skirt, or train of a wedding dress. It is heavier than Chantilly lace.

9. *Mermaid:* One of the more popular skirt styles, where the bodice is fitted and then flares from under the hips in a mermaid-tail fashion.

10. *Modesty piece:* A piece of fabric that is sewn into the middle of the neckline, especially a V-neck, to make it less revealing.

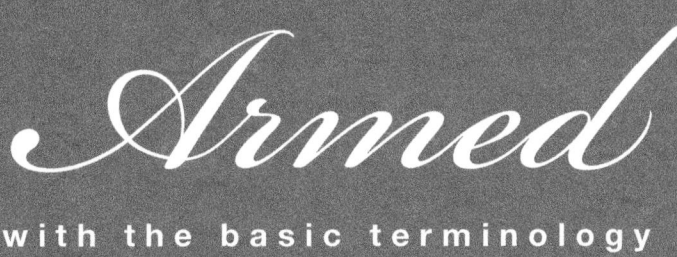

Armed with the basic terminology you are now ready...

Shall we go shopping?

Chapter Nine

SHOP TALK:
From Window Shopping to Your Walk Down the Aisle

When you were a little girl, did visions of your future wedding gown dance in your head? Now that you're engaged, you may be wondering how to select a dress that lives up to those long-ago dreams.

A wedding gown is so much more than just a dress. Your wedding gown tells a story; it speaks of who you are and how you came to this day. It is as unique as the person it is designed for. It is the dress you have always imagined walking down the aisle in.

Buying a wedding dress may be the most important and enduring style statement you'll ever make.

How's that for pressure?

After all, the gown you walk down the aisle in will be the true centerpiece of the day, probably the most expensive article of clothing you ever purchased, and the most talked-about thing you'll ever wear. It's a wardrobe milestone that you will remember forever.

Now that you are armed with information you need on the silhouettes that will flatter your body type most and are ready to go and try on wedding dresses to find "the one," do pay attention during the process for cues to how you would like your audience to relate to and remember you.

Your style is as unique as you and will reflect your personality. Which style reflects your truest self?

No matter what you might have imagined, it is a good idea to give this area serious thought. After all, you may not wish to just blend in with the masses. Or perhaps that *is* what you wish?

That is your choice . . .

As exciting and extraordinary as the experience of wedding gown shopping can be, it is one riddled with questions, regardless of whether you know what you want or not.

When should you start?

Where should you go?

What can you expect once you get there?

Relax. Don't get uptight. This should be a happy experience.

Allowing enough time to shop for and order your dress will help reduce anxiety.

Here are some tips before your start your bridal shopping spree, and remember, bridal consultants love to work with brides who understand and adhere to the basic rules when wedding shopping. To help them give you your best shopping experience, do the following:

- Arrive on time for your booked appointment so your bridal consultant can dedicate her time and effort to your service.

- Share your shortlist of styles and favorite dress features so your consultant can direct you toward the right gowns easily and doesn't have to haul a bunch of gowns into your dressing room that you will reject.

- Tell your consultant everything: the time and place of your wedding, what you do for a living, what you wear to parties, etc., so she can assess your personal style. If you're a minimalist, you aren't going to be comfortable in something really elaborate, and if you like to be fussy, then go with fussy. Sharing your information helps your consultant pull the right styles for you.

- Discuss your budget up front and ask questions about additional costs that may be involved such as alterations, accessories, and delivery as well as rush charges that may apply. Let your consultant know the maximum amount you can afford so that she does not show you dresses that are above your budget that, if you were to fall in love with, will make the rest of your choices pale in comparison and make you miserable.

- Limit your entourage to two or three close friends or relatives who will positively contribute to your shopping experience. Too many opinions can cause confusion and chaos and jeopardize your chances of making the right buying decision.

- Wear decent underwear to avoid any embarrassment for yourself and your consultant, who will be helping you get in and out of dresses.

- Bring the right undergarments and shoes to ensure the proper fit for the dresses you will be trying on.

- Keep your makeup light and take care to avoid staining the samples you are trying on.

- Ask for permission before you take pictures, as many bridal boutiques have a no-picture policy mainly to prevent the copying of designs and styles. Be courteous to their policies.

- Give honest feedback to your consultant about how you feel about a dress. By comparing your feedback on the different styles, your consultant will get to know your tastes and will be able to serve you better and help you find your dream dress.

- Shop with an open mind and be willing to try on different options, including ones you may have never considered. For now, don't be too particular about every little detail. Some dresses do not have hanger appeal but look fabulous on the body and vice versa. Being open will improve your chances of finding your dream dress. Besides, your consultant has seen a lot of bodies in a lot of gowns and may have something in mind you haven't thought of.

- Before you step foot in a bridal store, you should know the season, time, setting, and style of your wedding. Think about the theme and location of your wedding. Choose the time of day and formality of your wedding. All of these factors make a difference to your choice of gown.

Here's the timeframe and a checklist that will help:

TEN TO TWELVE MONTHS AHEAD

___*Choose your venue:* The venue you choose will dictate the style of dress you will wear for your walk down the aisle. A barefoot beach wedding and an extravagant ball gown do not go hand in hand. Definitely lock in your venue before you move forward with other plans.

___*Pick your wedding date:* This depends on your budget and desired place of your wedding, as well as the availability of your family and friends. Check whether the reception hall you want is available. Is it less costly in the winter than it is in the summer? If it is an outdoor wedding, weather will be a factor to consider. Or, you could pick a date that has a sentimental meaning to you—perhaps the anniversary date for when you first met.

___*Determine your gown budget:* Experts suggest allotting 8 to 15 percent of your wedding budget for your gown and accessories. The number can be massaged, however, depending on how important your dress is to you. Custom-ordered dresses cost more than off-the-rack gowns. Remember to factor in alteration costs as well.

___***Envision your dress.*** Think about your style and write down words that describe how you want to look and feel (elegant, royal, sweet, sexy, glamorous, etc.). Then, put into words what you absolutely do not want in a gown (sleeves, fitted skirt, full skirt, beading, lace, etc.).

___***Know your body:*** You have identified your body type and determined silhouettes that flatter you (see Chapter 5: Lines That Flatter: Choosing a Style for Your Figure). Use this knowledge.

___***Go armchair shopping:*** Browse through bridal magazines and websites to find designers and styles that appeal to you most. Think about weddings you have attended and wedding dresses that you have seen firsthand and recall whether any of those styles called out to you. Find out who the designers were.

___***Create an inspiration board:*** Use a corkboard, a folder, or an online inspiration board to organize your thoughts and ideas. Identify your favorites. This will allow you to collect your thoughts and get an actual look at your overall ideas, as well as serve as your inspiration and tool to help communicate your vision to your bridal consultant. Create a list of inspiring palettes and themes, silhouettes that inspire you, veils that appeal to you, accessories you would love to wear with your dress, invitation card ideas, bridesmaids' dresses, cakes, venues, reception décor, hair and makeup, bouquets and floral arrangements, table settings, centerpieces, party favors, photography, groom's and groomsmen's attire, and so much more. An inspiration board helps you focus and overcome confusion as you capture, sort through, eliminate, and organize your ideas. This allows you to share your ideas with your vendors and family, friends, and bridesmaids as well and get feedback before making a definite choice.

NINE TO TEN MONTHS AHEAD

___***Decide where to shop:*** Find a salon and a professional you like who can steer you in the right direction. Ask married friends where they purchased their gowns and what their experience was.

___***Don't limit yourself:*** Never walk into a bridal salon saying, "I don't want to wear . . ." If you try on only mermaid styles, you'll never discover that another style may actually work better for you. Remember, it doesn't cost anything to experiment, so take your cues from an expert. You want your wedding to be *you*, and an experienced bridal consultant can steer you in the right direction. Though your choices may be based on style, she'll focus on what's flattering. Ultimately, it is your choice, so just go with the flow for now.

___***Make appointments:*** Allow at least one to two hours per salon. Go in on a day when you're not stressed or rushed.

SALON 1:_____

DATE/TIME:_____

ADDRESS:_____

SALON 2:_____

DATE/TIME:_____

ADDRESS:_____

___***Buddy up and decide who to invite on your shopping spree:*** Choose a shopping companion whose style and opinion you trust—and who won't be pushy. There is no need to bring all of your wedding party along to help you choose your dress, either. Too many voices can make you lose sight of your vision. Everybody is going to have an opinion, whether helpful or not, so keep the size of your advice entourage to a minimum. If you bring a crowd, you'll end up trying on each person's favorite dress and you will be tired and confused by the end of the day. Remember, this is your day!

___***Get your gear ready to take with you:**_ When you shop, be sure to bring:

- a good bra and any shaping or support garments you plan to wear,
- control-top panty hose (eases dressing), and
- shoes with the same heel height you plan to wear at your wedding.

The above may not be the actual items you will wear, since the dress you end up choosing will impact the type of undergarments you will need. Many gowns have built-in corsets and bras, and if not, you can ask the store to have them sewn in as an option. As for shoes, the height of the heel you choose will determine the length of your gown, so remember to take a pair with the closest heel height to get a good feel for the overall look.

___***Go to your first appointment at each salon:**_ On your first shopping expedition, discover your most flattering silhouette based on your body type (for more on this process, see Chapter 5: Lines That Flatter: Choosing a Style for Your Figure). Once you see what works, look at a range of dresses in the silhouette that suits you. Whatever you do, make sure you stay true to your own personal style. If you're a non-traditionalist, you won't be happy with a puffy-sleeved, big ball gown, no matter how much your mom or best friend raves about it. This is not an impulse buy, so rather than putting down a deposit right away, take notes on the dresses that looked best on you and take pictures (if allowed) from different angles so you can step away and view them. Then rank the dresses in order of preference.

DESIGNER 1:_____

DESCRIPTION:_____

PRICE:_____RANK:_____

DESIGNER 2:_____

DESCRIPTION:_____

PRICE:_____RANK:_____

DESIGNER 3:_____

DESCRIPTION:_____

PRICE:_____RANK:_____

While you should have an overall concept for the wedding in mind when shopping for a gown, there is no need to make hairstyle decisions at this point. Generally, the headpiece is chosen to complement the gown, and then that will dictate how you wear your hair.

EIGHT TO NINE MONTHS AHEAD

___*Narrow down your dress choices and go for your next salon visit:* Try the dress that you ranked as your favorite.

When making your final choice, ask yourself the following questions:

1. Does this style flatter my figure?

2. Does the dress reflect my true personality?
3. Is the dress appropriate for the season?
4. Will the dress flow with the venue where I'm getting married?
5. Do I feel comfortable enough to walk gracefully down the aisle in this dress?
6. Does the dress fit within my overall dress budget, considering that I still need to purchase coordinating accessories, as well as factor in alteration costs?
7. Is this salon trustworthy?

At the salon, ask your salesperson the following questions:

1. Does the salon have an in-house alterations service?
2. If there is no in-house seamstress, does the store have any recommendations for alterations and fittings?
3. Are alterations included in the dress price? If not, then what extra charges will be incurred?
4. How many fittings will I need?
5. When will my dress arrive?
6. Does the gown have coordinating accessories such as veils, jewelry, and shoes? If so, try them on, too.

___***Be size wise:*** Forget your street wear size. Bridal designers and manufacturers size gowns differently, and consequently, wedding dresses run small. A size 6 in normal clothes is generally a size 10 in bridal, so do not be alarmed. If your wedding dress is not custom-made, it will be ordered to fit your largest measurement—whether it's bust, waist, or hips—and then taken in to fit everywhere else. The store will take your bust, waist, and hips measurements and consult the manufacturer's sizing chart and order the size that matches your largest measurement. So, if you end up buying a size that sounds too generous, don't worry. It's easier to make a dress smaller than to let it out.

Also note that wedding dresses come in one standard length, so if you need extra length, make sure to bring that to the store's attention. An extra charge may apply. This applies to larger sizes as well. As a general rule, wedding dresses larger than size 18 incur an extra charge. Calculate the cost and see if it is within the budget you have allocated.

SEVEN TO EIGHT MONTHS AHEAD

___***Order your wedding dress:*** The receipt should include:

- Designer name
- Style number or name
- Color, size, and measurement
- Approximate delivery date
- How many fittings are included in the price
- Amount of deposit, marked "paid"
- Balance owed for the gown
- Due date

FIVE MONTHS AHEAD

___***Decide what accessories you need:*** Veil, jewelry, headpiece, belt, jacket, wrap, bag, shoes, etc., that will coordinate with your dress and enhance the overall look to your satisfaction. The rule of thumb is to go with minimal and understated accessories if your gown is ornate, and vice versa if your gown is simple and clean-cut. Make your decision and your purchase.

___*Purchase your intimate apparel:*__ Now that you have found the dress, you can buy your wedding-day bra and underpinnings as well as your slip, as you'll need them for your fittings.

___*Make a fitness plan:*__ If you plan to lose weight, do so before the fittings begin.

___*Confirm delivery date:*__ Call the salon to make sure the delivery date still holds true.

If you plan to buy your wedding dress off the rack, then this is the time to purchase it.

If you are looking to purchase a sample gown or are waiting for a store sale, make sure you monitor closely when sales are announced. Let the store know to put you on their mailing list so you can be notified.

Some reputable designers have online stores where they offload samples as well as many brand-new but discontinued dresses that may be worth looking into.

Wedding gowns almost always need alterations, so make sure you factor the cost of alterations into your budget, whether purchasing it through a store or online.

TWO MONTHS AHEAD

___*Have your first fitting when your gown arrives*__: Invite a close friend along, one whose opinion you trust. Bring your accessories with you to experience the whole look. Unlike your first salon visit, when everyone's attention is on you, the first fitting is all about the dress. Bring the bra and shoes you plan to wear at the wedding and spend some time on your hair and makeup. You want to look and feel beautiful when trying on your dress for the first time. Your first fitting is where you make sure everything is exactly as ordered.

At the store, you'll go into a room and stand on a raised platform and your seamstress will start pinning your dress while you tell her how you'd like it to fit. Remember, the fit makes the dress, so be an active participant and don't feel intimidated if the fitter seems brusque. Your seamstress needs to know how much you'll be moving, whether you'll be walking through grass or on a hardwood floor. Will you be raising your arms a lot while dancing? If you plan on losing weight, then let her know that, too. Maybe you want extra padding in the bust, maybe you don't want a super-tight bodice. Whatever it is, make sure to express that during the pinning, because if you don't say anything, the seamstress will pin the dress the way most brides like it.

The dress's final fitting should be weeks before your wedding, so make sure to confirm that date. If you have all the accessories, then go ahead and try your dress with your veil, shoes, and jewelry to make sure everything is according to the order you placed.

FOUR TO SIX WEEKS AHEAD

___*Have your second fitting:* Make sure that:

- the hem skims the toes of your shoes,
- there is no wrinkling, bunching, or pulling, and
- your undergarments (bra, petticoat, etc.) work well with your dress.

Schedule fittings until you are satisfied.

Bring your maid or matron of honor to your final fitting to learn about the dress. Ask the salesperson to teach her how to bustle and button it.

TWO WEEKS AHEAD

___***Schedule your pick-up:*** Let the salon know when you will be picking up your dress. Try it one last time, especially if it's been a while since your last fitting, or if you have lost more weight.

___***Find a professional cleaner or preservation service:*** Find one that specializes in cleaning gowns for after the wedding.

THE DAY BEFORE

___***Do any necessary pressing and steaming:*** Smooth out the wrinkles and lay out all the accessories.

MORNING OF

___***Have a friend or bridesmaid inspect the gown:*** Look for any wrinkles or loose threads and for last-minute pressing needs.

___***Make sure a bridesmaid has a gown emergency kit ready:*** This should include safety pins, stain treatment, static remover, and so on.

LAST POSSIBLE MOMENT

___***Get dressed:*** Have someone help you slip into your undergarments and petticoat, slip into your dress, and step into your shoes. Put your veil on and find your bag and shawl.

LAST, BUT NOT LEAST

___***Prepare your gown if you will be traveling:*** If you're planning on heading directly from your wedding to your honeymoon, ask someone to prepare your gown for storage and either ship or drop it off to the cleaners as soon as possible since some stains, like red wine, can set permanently.

IN CONCLUSION . . .

With wedding dress fashion constantly evolving and hundreds of styles to choose from each season, the journey to finding your one dream dress can be utterly confusing. So, before you venture out, make sure of the following:

- You have a fairly good idea of your wedding details such as time of year and season, venue, and theme of your wedding.
- You have done extensive research, which includes identifying your body type and determining the silhouettes that flatter you (see Chapter 5: Lines That Flatter: *Choosing a Style for Your Figure*), browsed through websites and magazines to narrow down styles that will suit your figure, and made a list of stores or online retailers where you would like to shop.
- You have determined your dress budget and it includes variables such as alterations, extra charges for larger size or length requirements, and accessories such as headpiece, veil, shoes, jewelry, and undergarments.
- You have selected the companions who will accompany you on your shopping spree, and you understand that it would be best to limit this entourage to two or maximum three people whose opinion you respect and who are supportive of your choices.
- You have allotted a time when you are relaxed and focused rather than rushed to make a decision. Finding your ideal dress takes time and consideration and you really want to make an intelligent decision.
- You and your party have eaten before your journey. You'll be on your feet for a long time and the last thing you want is to get cranky because you are starving.

- You have chosen a well-established store or online retailer that carries the brand you are drawn to.
- You are open to suggestions from experts and willing to try on styles that you may not have picked otherwise. After all, there is no harm in being receptive to new ideas and feedback.
- You are going in with the right undergarments and shoes with the right heel height to try on your dress choices. You will get a better idea of the fit of a dress when you have these with you.
- You are aware that bridal sizing is not the same as ready-to-wear sizing and will not freak out about trying on a dress marked two sizes larger than you are used to wearing.
- Even if you are planning to lose weight before your wedding day, you are willing to place an order closer to your current weight. It is always safer to purchase a dress in your current size rather than a smaller one, as it is easier to take in the seams rather than let out in case you don't reach your desired weight.
- You will not be easily swayed by the opinions of others and are confident in your own choices and how you will feel when you have found **the** dress.
- When confused or in doubt, you will sleep on your choice before making your decision.

Trust your instincts. You automatically reach for the perfect dress to wear for your evening out, the perfect accessories to match. Why should it be any different when it comes to your wedding gown? Don't settle until you feel amazing, like the princess that you are. Be positive, straightforward, and confident as you're going through this part of your journey.

Yes, you can!

Chapter Ten

THE BUDGET-SAVVY BRIDE:
Online, Sale, or Rent?

Maybe the thought of spending more than two months' pay on a wedding dress never even occurred to you when you accepted the ring.

Just a few short years ago, finding a beautiful and elegant wedding dress would have required an all-hands-on-deck manhunt and a considerable amount of spare time and some change. Not so today. And seeing that time and money are very precious commodities, luxuries not everyone can afford, there are quite a few options for you to consider when looking for an incredibly memorable wedding dress.

Whether you're looking for an unfussy gown for your beach wedding, trying to find a lace-adorned midi dress to wear to City Hall, or you're going all out but still want something spectacular, there are so many options for you today to realize your dream.

Here are some of them:

ONLINE PURCHASE

Like the rest of the fashion industry, the bridal world, too, is experiencing change. Many reputable designers have adopted the digital trend and are now offering their designs online.

Can you really get a wedding gown delivered to your doorstep? Yes, absolutely.

For many brides, the ability to purchase designer gowns in this most effortless way is a dream come true. Often the prices offered online are considerably lower than the dresses sold in stores due to lower overhead costs to designers, which affords savings to you, the bride.

One thing to bear in mind is that some online bridal stores offer a try-on option, while others do not. If it is a brand that you are familiar with and which has a good reputation, then there should be no need to worry. Do your homework and check the seller's policies and procedures.

Today, an ocean of choices has become available online, which can often overwhelm and cause confusion.

Here are ten steps you can take to make your choice easier:

1. Make a list of the features you wish for in a dress that would look good on your body type such as silhouette, neckline, sleeves, and fabric. Also list what you would like to avoid (read Chapter 5: Lines That Flatter: *Choosing a Style for Your Figure* and *Chapter 6: Wedding Dress Silhouettes*).

2. Filter by price to make sure you're staying within your dress budget.

3. Pick out a number of gowns that fit the aforementioned criteria.

4. Pin these on your online inspiration board or print them out so you can lay them all out and compare them.
5. Eliminate the dresses that do not match your needs.
6. Pay attention to details on the chosen dresses: note the fabric, construction, and how it drapes on the model.
7. Get help from those whose opinion you trust and make your decision.
8. Check the manufacturer's measurement chart and determine the optimal size.
9. Place your order.
10. Find a good seamstress who has experience working with complicated gowns. Once your dress arrives, you will more than likely need some alterations.

Unfortunately, in this day and age, the Internet is flooded with websites selling cheap imitations and fake goods, some even bold enough to use other designers' original images to lure you into believing that you are, in fact, receiving an authentic designer dress. So, beware of some sites that offer bargain dresses. Sometimes a cheap dress can just end up being a headache and cost more than you bargained for.

It is best to order directly from a designer's website than from third-party vendors or those who pose as representatives. When a designer puts their name on a piece, it is a symbol of pride, and they are putting their reputation on the line. Investing in a reputable designer's piece ensures that you are receiving a well-made garment of the best quality, an heirloom that you can pass on to generations.

SAMPLE AND CLEARANCE SALES

Most bridal salons have seasonal sample and clearance sales to make room for new merchandise as well as to get rid of discontinued styles due to lack of space and changing demands. This is your chance to purchase a fabulous gown sans the hefty price.

Since wedding dresses are sized differently compared to ready-to-wear clothing, make sure you know where you are on the size chart prior to purchasing your sale gown, as most sales are final.

In most cases, though, the store may not have the size or the color you need. Floor samples are usually smaller in size and have been tried on by several brides-to-be, so expect some wear and tear.

A sale is only good if you are flexible and willing to settle for whatever you can get. Most stores do not disclose which styles and sizes they will be offering for sale. Also, don't expect to find the current year and season's models, as they would not be among the sale items.

Call the stores where you found some styles you liked to see if and when they will be having their sales. Plan in advance so you don't get caught up in the mayhem, as it can get quite chaotic as others are also there searching for their dream gown at a bargain price. Some stores require an appointment, so do your homework.

Here are ten steps you can take to pick the right dress with minimum hassle:

1. Visit the bridal salons in advance to find out what choices are being offered. Try on several dresses and shortlist a few that you love.

2. Note the dress model numbers and sizes so that you reach them first on the day of the sale.

3. Get your friends to pitch in and help to scout out the potential gowns faster by showing them pictures of styles you are looking for.

4. Dressing rooms can be rushed and chaotic during sales, so don't expect to spend too much time trying on one gown after another.
5. Be ready to make a quick decision and get ready to make your purchase there and then.
6. Expect that this is a final sale.
7. In the event that the dress is not in your size, ask the store if they offer alterations and the costs involved.
8. Make an appointment to bring the dress back for alterations and fittings.
9. If your sample gown is soiled from dirt and sweat from having been tried on, then you may need to get it cleaned. Ask the store for their recommendations.
10. Factor in alteration and cleaning costs and make sure you are within your budget.

Unfortunately, if you have only a single style in mind, then your chances are not so good and a sale is not the answer to finding the dress of your dreams.

RENTING YOUR GOWN

Bridal gowns can be expensive to purchase and unfortunately not every bride can afford to make that commitment.

Rather than settling for a cheap dress that fits your budget, consider renting your chosen wedding gown for a fraction of the price you would normally pay to purchase it.

As more bridal rental places pop up, many brides find themselves opting to wear a pre-loved dress on their wedding day, either because they cannot afford to purchase or do not consider it worthwhile to invest in a dress that they will wear only once in a lifetime. Or, it could be because they are environmentally conscious or even that they have no room to store the dress after the ceremony. Of course, this also means that the dress will not have the honor of being passed on as an heirloom piece.

When renting a dress, please keep the following four tips in mind:

1. ***Choose a reliable bridal shop***: Check out the references and testimonials from brides who have experienced the store's services. Online reviews and feedback are a good indication that the store is reliable and dependable.

2. ***Ask for an all-inclusive package:*** Before you sign the contract, make sure the price includes alterations such as taking in or letting out the bodice, adjusting hemlines, and adding a bustle.

3. ***Read the contract:*** Make sure to read between the lines. Check the clauses on the number of days you're allowed to keep the dress, whether it has to be cleaned before being returned, damage charges if any, pick-up and return dates, late charges, etc. Discuss the parts you're not clear about before signing on the dotted line.

4. ***Ask for matching accessories and veil:*** Most rental stores will have veils for rent, so ask for one that will match your dress. If you have your own jewelry, then great, but if not, the store may have matching accessories for you to rent as well.

Whatever

option you choose,

you can be wed looking

as grand as you

always dreamt

you would!

CHAPTER ELEVEN

COLOR IN YOUR WEDDING

When everyone around you is wearing white, why not choose a wedding gown in a different color and make a statement?

Be bold with color.

When I launched my first bridal collection, St. Pucchi, in 1985, my entire collection of sixteen pieces was in color. At a time when the American bride wore only white, I had not designed a single white dress. I had absolutely no clue that color would not be accepted and was traumatized by the initial thought that perhaps I had failed. However, three days into my first bridal show in Dallas, I was featured on the front page of the *Dallas Apparel News* and hailed as a pioneer for introducing color to the American bridal scene. The US bridal landscape was never the same again!

The tradition of a white wedding gown began in earnest following Queen Victoria's marriage in 1840. Up until then, a bride married in gowns of various fashionable colors. Contrary to modern belief, white bridal dresses were never a sign of purity, but in fact reflected the social status of a woman who could afford to be married in a white dress that she would only wear once in her lifetime. Queen Victoria single-handedly set the trend, and the ideal of the white wedding was now firmly in place.

White became an emblem of innocence and purity of girlhood. Thus, the attachment to virtue was created, and every bride wanted to be thought virtuous. While not always entirely accurate, this reference highlights how deeply instilled the image of the bride in white had become. White, in all its classical purity, was the universally favored color for wedding dresses.

Nevertheless, the white dress is not for every bride. With so many shades of white, thought must be given to the becomingness of the shade, since there are so many tones in white. What suits the pale blond may be absolutely unbecoming on a rosy brunette.

Today's modern bride has realized that she has options, and is free to be married in the style and color that best suits her personality, taste, and appearance. After all, this is her day, one that she will remember for the rest of her life.

Below are the popular bridal color options:

Beige: This is a neutral color. It is basically a pastel form of brown.

Blush: This is the palest pink color. Very popular and complements almost all skin tones.

Butterscotch: *Similar to soft peach, but with a* light golden-brown hue that looks deliciously rich, and complements other color palettes beautifully.

Champagne: This color can range among various very pale tints of yellow-orange that are close to beige. The name is derived from the typical color of the beverage champagne.

Diamond white/Silk white/Natural white: The brightest white that can be found in a natural fiber, like silk. It usually has a warm, creamy undertone and is flattering on all skin tones.

Ecru: *A greyish* pale yellow or a light greyish, yellowish brown. It is often used to describe colors in such fabrics as silk and linen. "Ecru" is a French word, meaning unbleached or raw. It's very similar to beige.

Gold: One of the hottest new bridal colors, gold is ideal for warm-complexioned women. It comes in various hues, so try and pick the lightest and softest shade of gold. Gold thread is commonly used in embroideries, and accents on gowns such as sashes and flowers.

Ivory: There are many shades of ivory, which may vary from off-white to creamy yellow-ivory.

Platinum: Similar to silver, but with a hint of soft gray. A very popular color in couture bridal gowns, as well as used as accents such as flowers and sashes.

Stark white: The whitest white found only in synthetic fabrics like polyester blends, this color can have a hint of grey or blue, and can be a challenge to choose from. Some bright shades of whites may look unflattering, so care must be taken when choosing the right shade.

Custom colors: Mint-green, blue, ruby, black, etc. are other colors that have been used in bridal.

Today, more and more brides are opting to wear colored bridal gowns. The traditional rule of just white or ivory for your wedding dress is totally outdated.

Sometimes theme weddings call for colors that are outside the bridal norm. At other times, these colors are used as accents as well. For instance, you could add splashes of color with a silk sash, contrast beading on your dress, or make a bold statement with colored heels.

So, if you know that white doesn't suit you, don't try to make it fit. Opt for a color that is more flattering rather than going with what you believe is expected of you. The right color can add instant opulence to your wedding attire, from head to toe.

Whatever color you choose, remember that a color you see inside a bridal salon may look different once you're wearing it at your venue. Different light spectrums will change the color of your dress, even if only slightly. Take your gown into natural light to make sure you like it. Better to be safe than sorry.

Weddings are personal. Do what feels true to you.

Regardless of what color you choose to wear, make sure it is an expression of your individual style, and just enjoy!

THE WEDDING COLORS

Having decided the color of your dress, the rest of your wedding colors are easier to plan.

What are your favorite colors?

Think about the hues you love, as well as those you dislike. Take a nuanced approach to how you will use color. Find something to inspire you throughout the design process. Maybe it's a place, either real or imagined. Or a mood: serene and uplifting. Perhaps a painting that moves you.

What color combination would you like to use to help make your day beautiful and special, one that will dazzle all? Create a color palette.

The colors you are drawn to reflect your personality, tell the world what kind of person you are, and affects what you wish to communicate, so it's important to choose colors wisely.

Take a look at some of the hues below and find out how to identify the shades that complement the person you are. Then gather different shades of each color that calls to you together to see how they may fit into the color scheme of your wedding:

RICH RUBY RED
Keywords: Excitement/Love/Passion/Power

Ruby is an emotionally charged color representing romance, strong feelings, and passion. It hints at strength and determination, so when you choose this hue, it may mean that you're looking for fire or energy in your life, since red tones are recognized for their ability to stimulate the senses.

LILAC/PURPLE
Keywords: Creativity/Sensuality/Spirituality/Peace of Mind

Sensual and mysterious, spiritual and intuitive, lilac and purple shades combine the excitement and passion of red tones with the peaceful tranquility of blue. Their meditative, soul-searching qualities help us overcome our fears and focus on the important aspects of life.

BLUE
Keywords: Calmness/Confidence/Strength/Trust

Blue hues are known for inspiring feelings of calmness, confidence, reliability, and security and evoke the timeless beauty of endless seas and summer skies. The color inspires feelings of relaxation and promotes peacefulness, trust, honesty, and loyalty, and also helps calm the senses.

Green
Keywords: Nature/Balance/Harmony/Life/Vitality

Signifying nature and new beginnings, green stands for renewal and health. Its powerful attributes help to ground us, refreshing and regenerating our minds. Light greens are particularly energetic, evoking the spirit of nature. They have a soothing, healing effect on the whole body and are a useful means of keeping yourself grounded.

TOPAZ
Keywords: Energy/Happiness/Illumination/Joy

Energetic and joyful, topaz expresses the sun's brightness, warmth, and light. It's the color of ideas and dreams, stimulating creativity and boosting confidence, as well as clearing the mind, reviving the spirit, and encouraging us to live life to the fullest.

PEACH
Keywords: Compassion/Innocence/Peacefulness/Romance

Peach is a versatile tone that helps create a deep sense of personal fulfillment and contentment. With its peaceful air and hint of romance, it can play a powerful role where emotional healing is required.

PINK
Keywords: Excitement/Passion/Playfulness/Drama

With its sense of passion and playfulness, choosing this hue highlights a sensual, yet confident and vibrant nature. The depth of pink will also stimulate the senses and unleash hidden energy.

ORANGE
Keywords: Cheerfulness/Enthusiasm/Fun/Warmth

This juicy, summery shade is wonderfully energizing. Sunrise orange evokes love of the glow of golden sunlight and is a vivacious color that brings clarity and creativity and promotes physical strength and endurance. It also implies a desire for a fresh and playful element in your life.

Here are ten tips to help you choose your winning colors:

1. Start off by choosing from the above list your five favorite colors. You can pull up the shades closest to your choices online from Pantone (a collection of colors most graphic designers and artists use) so you can see all the different hues and narrow down the shades you are drawn to. Print these out and line them up.

2. Get a swatch of the color of your dress from your bridal salon and add this to the line-up. Do they look good together?

3. Slowly go through your list of the different elements of your wedding: your cake, your flowers, the décor, the bridesmaids' dresses, the mother of the bride's dress . . . Can you picture them in any of the colors in the line-up?

4. Do these colors reflect the mood and the aura you have visualized for your wedding? Imagine how you would like your wedding guests to feel at your wedding. Are you wishing to set a romantic mood, or is it a high-energy party? Do your colors create and evoke those feelings?

5. Once you have narrowed down the colors you prefer most, go to the florist and see what flowers in your chosen colors are in season during the time of your wedding. Have the florist create a small bouquet of the color combination and see how you like it.

6. Go to the salon where you will be ordering your bridesmaids' dresses and select the styles you like most and see if that manufacturer offers them in any of your chosen colors. Get a swatch from the store and add it to the line-up.

7. Next, go to the baker where you will be ordering your cake and look at the choices available. Decide the type of cake and which of the colors you have chosen would look best. Your wedding's color combination can be easily incorporated into the icing on your cake.

8. Décor is the last step, because décor accents come in all colors of the rainbow and you can pick and choose what you want. If you have chosen the theme of your day, then have your decorator introduce the color combinations you finalize.

9. Lay out a full table design to see your palette come to life in full color before you get too far along in your planning. Do you absolutely love it?

10. Having determined your overall color palette and design, convey it to your vendors. If the process is too overwhelming, seek the help of an event designer, floral designer, or a trusted group of friends.

This

is your day.

Trust your instincts.

Pick the wedding colors

you love most, ones

that reflect

your personality.

Have Fun!

Chapter Twelve

IS NUDE THE NEW WHITE?

There is so much pressure for brides today to have a perfect body!

Plastic surgeons are making tons of money sculpting bodies so women can wear nude dresses. Runway nudity has been taken to a new extreme, and sheer fashion and styles have continued to memorialize many celebrities in the last year or so, leaving a scant bit left to the imagination.

Dangerously low necklines, slits cut up to here, necklines inviting nip slips, and sheer butt panels are all too common, and no one feels exploited any more. It's clear that many women are giving their underwear a night off and going commando.

While these show-stopping moments are practically taken for granted on the red carpet, we would be remiss not to wonder whether modern brides-to-be envision a similar look for their walk down the aisle on their most important day.

There are arguably two schools of bridal fashion—modernist and romantic. I would like to think that my St. Pucchi designs represent the latter, not just in the silhouettes and decorative approaches, but in the whole narratives woven around my collections. There is something incredibly poetic about the clothes that I design—heavily thematic, ever-changing.

Personally, I like a little bit of sheer delight, peek-a-boo, or strategically placed cut-outs.

Years ago, I introduced a dress that had a sheer net base and embroidered leaves in various sizes placed strategically to hide sensitive areas. People were shocked! Eventually, the dress was dubbed the Adam and Eve dress!

Then there was the dress that I designed for country-western singer-songwriter Alison Krauss that had a very sheer Chantilly lace bottom that she wore to the CMA awards in New York. The photographers went wild!

We have come a long way since then. St. Pucchi dresses are revealing, yet they conceal at the same time. I continue to show plunging necklines, but not so low that they leave nothing to the imagination.

Always leave something for the imagination. Bridal fashion, after all, is about fantasy, about living your dream . . .

There is a way to do a sheer dress that doesn't require showing every inch of flesh. The trick I employ when designing for those who insist on the nude look is to use deceptive flesh-color lining that provides the same nude feel without the added fuss, and is wearable and appropriate.

In fact, the brides who make a lasting impression manage to steer clear of the nude trends in favor of a relatively more demure approach that promises to stand the test of time.

I would like to see bridal fashion return to glamour and away from the look of lingerie.

It's time for something new.

Let's retire the naked dress and return to wearing real clothes, and send a message to future generations that looking classic is forever, adds real soul, and is magnetically beautiful.

Showing less skin can be enticing. Having someone wonder what is underneath, having a little mystery and leaving something to the imagination? Priceless!

One thing is for sure: with great style comes great responsibility. It is up to you to set an example for future generations.

Your wedding is captured in photos that you will want to show off in years to come— to your children, your grandchildren . . .

How do you want to be remembered?

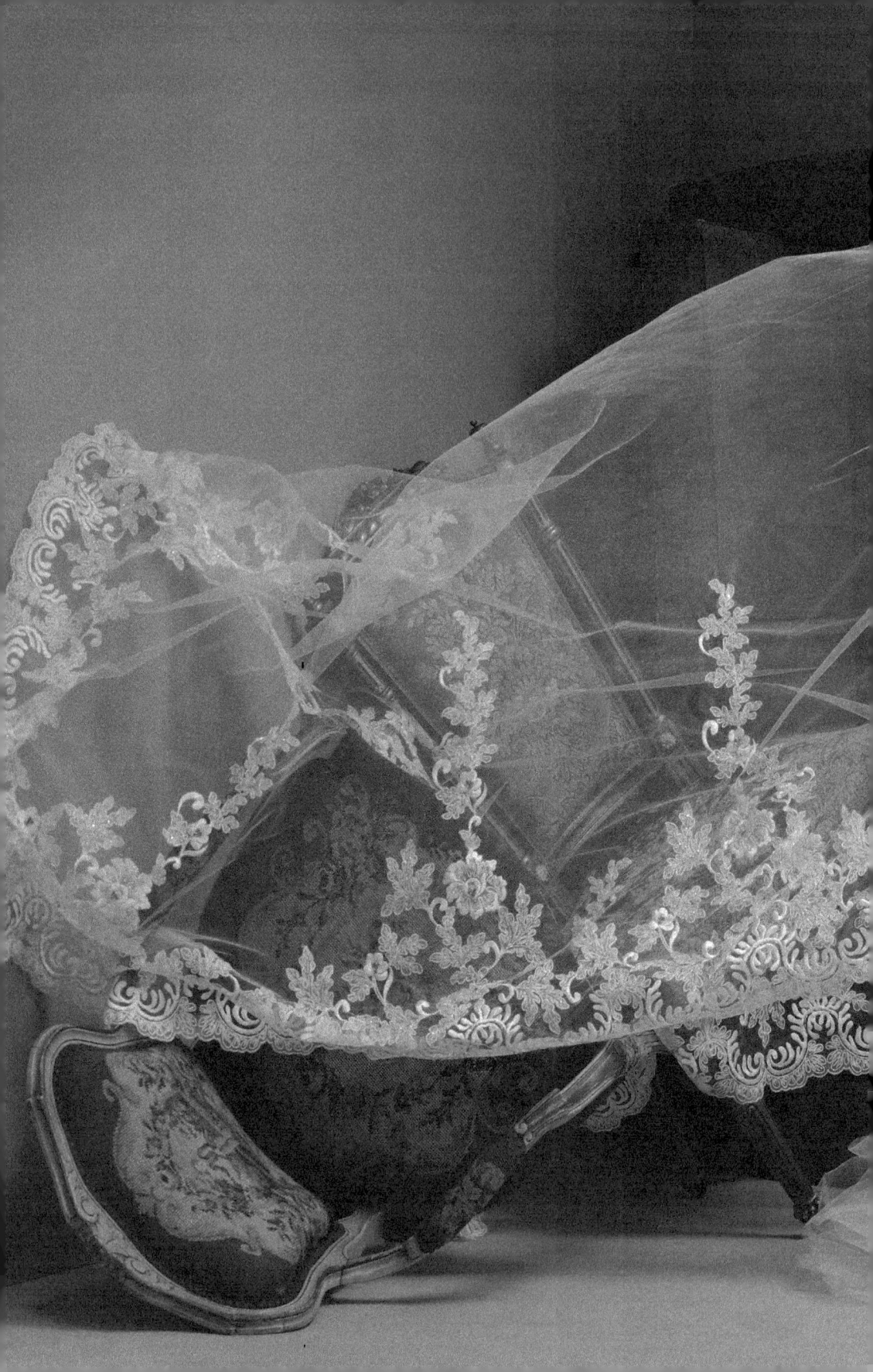

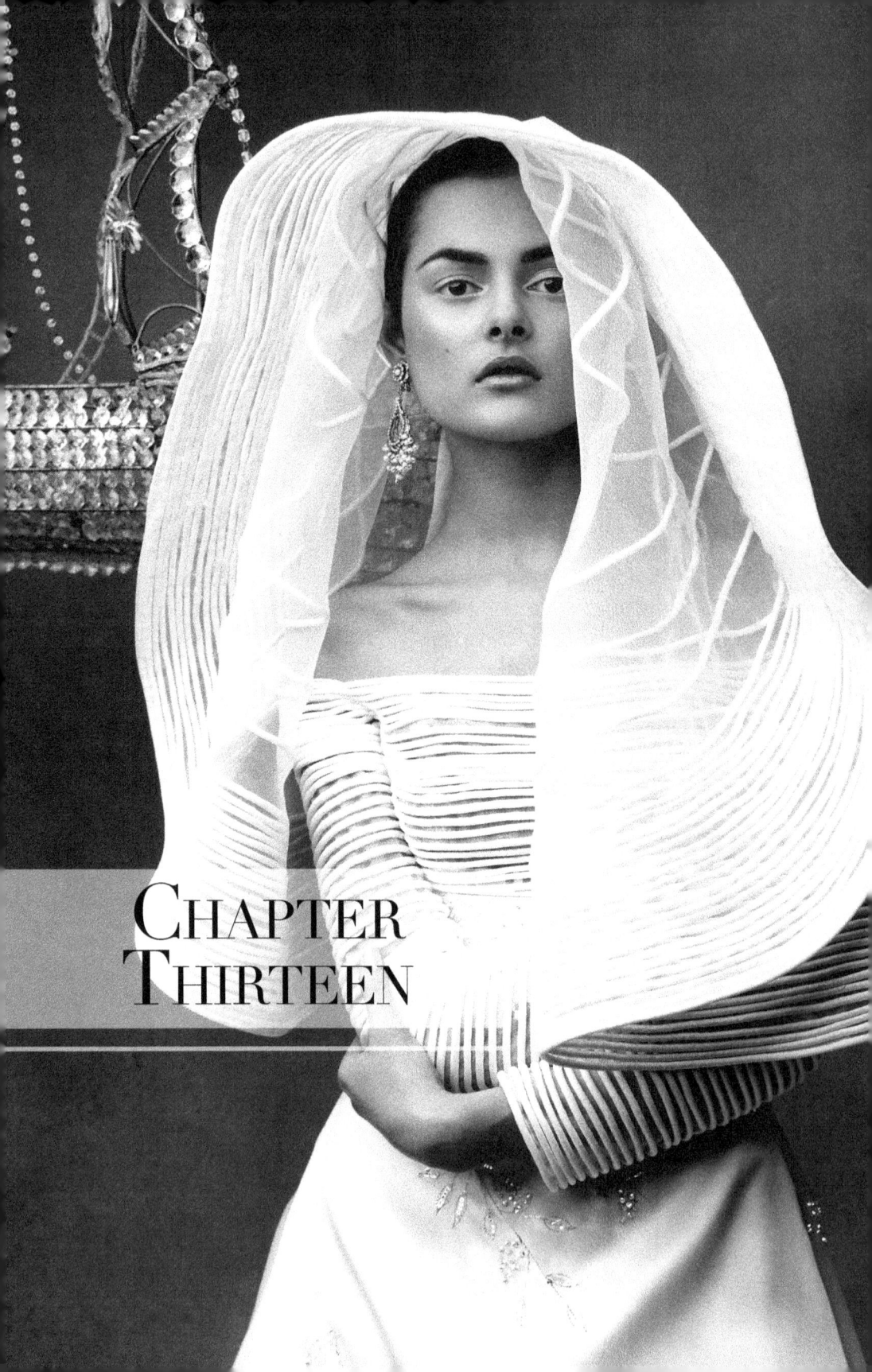

Chapter Thirteen

THE CROWNING GLORY: *The Veil*

Every bride following the Victorian era gave the utmost importance to the veil. It was the most important part of a bride's costume.

The veil was sacrosanct and was attached even to the bonnet if that was the look that she was going for. Veil choices came in various fabrics, such as silver-flecked tulle and white crisp lisse—very full tulle veils were the most common and the least expensive.

Lace veils were the most coveted, although more expensive than other options. It became very popular to wear an heirloom veil as something "borrowed."

Tulle veils, very full, were worn more than any other in the nineteenth century. The veil was the most necessary part of a bride's costume. Typically, the diaphanous veils of lace and tulle were worn at the back of the bride's head, fastened to a wreath of roses and myrtle, to match their neoclassic gowns.

The perfect veil can add an extraordinary touch, giving a particular grace and delicacy to the face and figure. Often the final touch, a veil can make a great difference in influencing brides when making a choice on their wedding dress. No matter how short or long, it completes the look and creates an air of mystery around the bride's face.

It is not necessary to keep a veil on after the ceremony, which is why there are options of detachable veils. The shorter the dress, the longer the veil, is my opinion.

Most veils today are made of illusion or tulle, but some are also made of English net and organza.

Here are the popular veil styles:

Angel: Generally worn with contemporary, minimalist gowns, this is a flat, square-cut, ungathered veil.

Ballerina/Ballet: Slightly longer than the fingertip-length. It is very manageable.

Birdcage: Ideal for a vintage look. The veil is generally stiff, made of sheer wide-mesh veiling with gently shirred sides, either covering the face and ears to just below the chin, or slanted to cover the nose ending to the side of the chin. The birdcage veil is usually attached to decorative combs or hats.

Blusher: For a traditional look, add a blusher. This is a loose, single short veil worn forward over the face. It conceals the face as the bride walks down the aisle and is lifted up by the groom as he kisses the bride. The blusher is usually attached in back to a longer or tiered veil, or on a separate comb so as to be removable.

Cascade: Two or more layers of veiling cascading down the back.

Cathedral: Think princess. This veil cascades three and a half yards from the headpiece or comb, and is usually worn with dresses that have a cathedral train.

Chapel: Veiling that measures two and a half yards in length from headpiece or comb.

Circular veil: Cut in a circle, this veil has no gathers and attaches to the head with a comb. It can come in any length.

Elbow: A veil that falls to the elbow for a laid-back look. Often paired with a ball gown to help balance out a fuller skirt.

Fingertip: This length is a favorite among brides and appropriate for any kind of dress, gracefully touching the fingertips when the arms are held straight at the sides.

Floor-length: Veiling cut to touch the floor, usually to the same length as a floor-length dress.

Fly-away/Informal: A multi-layered, shoulder-length veil, usually worn with informal dresses or styles with open or decorative backs that are too pretty to be covered.

Mantilla: Think old-world elegance. Long, made of tulle, lace, or lace-trimmed, this veil is often draped over the head and secured by a comb.

Pouf: Small gathered cluster of veiling connected to a headpiece, usually worn with an informal dress.

Royal: An extra-long veil that extends to meet the royal-length train.

Tiered: This choice connects several layers in different lengths together. It can be versatile, often with detachable layers for different looks.

Waltz: *This veil tends to fall anywhere between the knee and the mantle.*

Waterfall: *A multi-layered veil that touches the shoulders.*

Finishes and Trims

There are several finishes to the veil. Some have rolled edges or are machine-edged, some are edged with ribbons in various widths, and others are not edged at all. Some are enhanced with embroidery, often to match the bride's dress, and yet others are beaded or scattered with crystals. The options are endless. Here are a few:

Cut: The veiling material is cut, but not sewn.

Lettuce: A "bunched up" stitch that gives the effect of a lettuce leaf, all the way around the edge of the veiling

Merrow: A rolled or stitched edge known as overlock sewing, this gives a defined effect to the veil.

Ribbon: Thin silk or satin ribbon sewn along the edge of the veil all the way around.

Rolled: A machine zigzag stitch that helps roll the veiling edge to give an effect similar to a ribbon edge.

Scalloped: Instead of a straight cut, the edges of the veil are cut in repeated patterns of a "U" or half-moons.

Painters have always been fascinated by the bridal veil . . . In my opinion, no bridal ensemble is complete without the veil.

FINISHING TOUCHES:
Embellishments and Accessories

Nearly every dress in a storied bridal boutique has some sort of detailing to speak of: an inordinate amount of Swarovski crystals, crazy-intricate beading, or a bustle that requires half your extended family to tame.

What is a wedding dress without its embellishments? A wedding dress can be made from the best fabrics and most flattering cut, but without embellishments to spruce it up, it is somehow incomplete.

With so many options, it's hard to know where to begin. Suffice it to say that embellishments are meant to draw attention to your best features while camouflaging areas you're not so thrilled about, all without overwhelming you or your dress.

EMBELLISHMENTS

The following are a few embellishments to help spruce up your creation and to give it a unique spin that is all your own.

Buttons: Decorative or functional, buttons add a traditional feel as well as pizzazz to a wedding dress. They are generally placed at the back of the dress, over the zipper or with loops, or at the edge of long sleeves. Also popular are buttons lining up the entire back seam of the skirt, along the length of the train. They can be silk-covered, beaded, crystalized, or even in color to add emphasis to the dress.

Edging: Edging can be any kind of lace, embroidery, ribbon, or cording that helps give the final touch to your design. Edging can be sewn on the sleeves, at the hem of the skirt, and around the neckline, as well as around the veil to give it a finished look. It also adds value to the dress.

Fabric flowers: Multi-dimensional, monotone or colored, fabric flowers and leaves are popular on bridal gowns. They can be placed either in clusters or individually on the shoulders, at the back, on one side of the waist, or spread over the skirt to give a vintage look. The most popular are silk rosettes. The size and shape of these flowers determines the overall visual impact it will have on the dress.

Beads, sequins, and pearls: Beads can be either glass or plastic and add a soft texture to your dress. Pearls are more traditional and come in various sizes, of which the most precious are seed pearls and freshwater pearls, which when sewn on help give dimension to the lace or embroidery of your dress. Sequins are small, iridescent plastic discs that add shine and texture.

Crystals and rhinestones: Swarovski is the best-known brand in crystals. Crystals come in various shapes and sizes as well as an assortment of colors. They add dimension and add value to the lace or embroidery of a wedding dress. Rhinestones are imitation crystals generally used to ornament fabrics on the dress or veil to add shine.

ACCESSORIES

Now that you have your dress, the next step is to choose your accessories. Bridal accessories are key to completing your transformation into a gorgeous bride. Of course, these must complement your wedding dress so be mindful not to overdo it.

If your dress is already rich in details and comes complete with ornate embellishments, then keep your accessories simple. On the other side of the spectrum, if your dress is clean and simple, by all means dress it up with bold jewelry and a headpiece.

Plan the overall look you want to achieve before going accessory shopping. Here are a few key components that will enhance your wedding day look:

JEWELRY

While you may not use your wedding dress after your wedding day, you will most likely be able to use your wedding jewelry on future occasions, which makes this a worthwhile investment.

Your jewelry need not match your wedding ring but should go with the theme of your wedding and the style of your dress. With so many options available, it can be confusing. The main thing to be mindful of is that the base metal should complement your wedding gown's shade and the pattern should come together beautifully with the design of your dress. Keep the metals uniform throughout your attire. For instance, if your dress has silver accents, then go with silver jewelry, or use gold when there are gold or warm accents.

Your jewelry should reflect your personal style and taste, so choose colors and designs that you are comfortable wearing and feel great in. Just because your wedding dress is white, you need not restrict your choices to pearls and diamonds. Beautiful trinkets with colored stones and gems will add a pop of color to your wedding day ensemble.

The key is to remember that balance is key where wedding jewelry is concerned. If your dress has many details, then avoid too much jewelry and stick with the basics like a pair of earrings and a bracelet. A bold necklace is appropriate if you're wearing a strapless dress that is simpler on the top, and when worn with a statement ring.

Just don't overdo it.

Shoes

When it comes to shoes, comfort is key. Remember, it will be a long day, and you will be on your feet much of the time. There is nothing worse than feet that hurt. What heel height can you comfortably carry? Go with those. One option is to find shoes with platform heels that are gentler on your arches. Your shoes can be adorned with lace or can even be in color to add flair and spunk. Wear appropriate shoes for the venue. For instance, if it is a garden wedding, you may want flats, as heels can get caught up in the dirt and be uncomfortable to manage.

GLOVES

Gloves add an old-world elegance to wedding attire. The question is, what's appropriate and what's not?

Here are the general rules:

Long gloves: For a longer, more formal dress, gloves of either elbow or opera length (above the elbow) give an elegant look. They draw attention to your arms, especially if your shoulders are bare and you have on a sleeveless dress or one with spaghetti straps. Opera-length gloves also provide warmth and flair if you're having a winter wedding.

Short gloves: These are great when wanting to create a subtler effect. For a summer garden wedding, short gloves lend a fresh and light flavor and give your gown a daintier, less formal look.

If you have heavy arms, gloves will call attention to them, rather than camouflage them. If you have short arms but love the look of a long glove, choose an elbow-length pair rather than opera-length. Stay away from gloves that cut your upper arm at its heaviest point.

Leather can be worn year-round, but save velvet gloves for winter.

When wearing a suit jacket with a skirt or pants, gloves should be classic and simple. Forget wide cuffs and embellished trim. Short, wide kid gloves look best with suits.

A fashion-forward bride can pair her gown with a colored glove, perhaps an ice-blue or a lilac that coordinates with her bridesmaids' dresses.

Cover-Ups

Tradition and weather sometimes require that the bride wear a garment to cover her bare shoulders, warm her neck, or cloak herself to fend off the cold, especially when wearing a strapless or sleeveless dress.

The following are some outerwear options:

Bolero: A cropped, long-sleeved, simply structured jacket that ends just below the bust line, often open in the front with no fasteners. A sheer bolero jacket provides enough coverage for church.

Cape: A triangular-shaped garment, armless, with or without a hood, that slips over and hangs from the shoulders. It may have front closures, and can be as long as the train or the dress.

Capelet: Same as the cape but a much shorter version, some so short as to appear to be a collar.

Jacket: A cover-up that depends on the style of your dress, the jacket can come in many variations such as a tuxedo jacket, a blazer, or peplum style flaring at the waist.

Shrug: Comprised of two long sleeves that meet at the back, with little or no fabric visible in the front of the bodice.

Stole: A relatively narrow, rectangular piece of fabric that is meant

to be thrown over the shoulders or wrapped and draped around the upper body and neck.

Veil: Veils give a particular grace and delicacy to the face and figure. There are many options to choose from, but bear in mind that your veil must complement your dress as well as be appropriate for your venue. For instance, you would not wear a cathedral veil if you're having a beach or garden wedding. A short or cage veil may be more appropriate for these settings. At the same time, you may not want to wear a cage veil for a cathedral wedding where a chapel-length or cathedral-length veil may be more fitting (See Chapter 13: The Crowning Glory: *The Veil* for more details).

Even the simplest bridal gown has its unique embellishments to make it stand out. Each design must carefully use the right decorations to make sure they sit together in perfect unison.

One thing to keep in mind — embellishments should add to, not take away from, your dress.

Chapter Fifteen

ALL ABOUT THE BUSTLE

By the end of the 1870s, hooped skirts were no longer stylish, and fashionable women opted instead for gowns with elaborate bustles.

A bustle is the name given to the art of drawing up the train so that the gown can become floor-length and allow the bride to move around after the ceremony with ease and avoid tripping. It also ensures that the gown does not drag around on the ground after the ceremony and get soiled. To accomplish this, the train can be pinned up and secured by hidden hooks on the back of the dress.

A bustle is useful when the bride chooses a dress with a train. Many brides love the formality of a wedding gown with a long train, but it can be cumbersome at the reception.

Assuming that the bridal gown you have purchased has a train, it will need to be bustled after the ceremony and before the reception, resulting in a floor-length dress that is easier to walk and dance in.

All dresses with trains from the smallest sweep to the grandest cathedral can benefit from a proper bustle. Depending on the length of the train, a dress can be bustled by lifting and tucking the extra fabric underneath or over the skirt. Larger trains may need to be folded up using a system of hooks.

A bustle is a unique and amazing creation that not only serves a practical purpose, but also adds tremendous style and interest to the bridal gown.

There are two basic types of bustles: the traditional bustle, and the French bustle. Each look is a little different, but both serve the same purpose, and work well with all types of trains.

Traditional bustle: Also known as the over-bustle, this type of bustle is recommended for gowns with waistlines. It is created by gathering up the train and securing it with buttons or hooks and loop attachments at points on the waistline or elsewhere on the back of the gown for a cascading effect. This is an excellent choice for gowns carrying extensive embroideries or laces, as it allows a new configuration to be created to showcase the details and embroidery in a different light. Generally, lace appliques, bows, or rosettes are added to hide the attachments and to provide extra support, to allow the bustle to stay in place.

French bustle: Also known as the under-bustle, this is the most popular type of bustle and is appropriate for all types of gowns. It is more elaborate and can seem almost Victorian on many dresses. With the French bustle, the buttons and loops or ribbons are attached to the underside of the skirt and train so that the train is actually tucked underneath and pinned or hooked to the fabric of the dress that way.

When the ribbons of the skirt are tied to the corresponding ribbons of the train, the excess fabric of the train is drawn under the skirt, allowing the top fabric of the train to nestle over the train in a pillow-like fashion, adding a whole new look to the overall dress.

Depending on the length and width of the train, as well as the weight, the number of bustle points may vary anywhere from five to fifteen.

Choosing a bustle style depends on the dress and your taste. The important thing to bear in mind is that the gown, after it is bustled, shows off the beauty of the embroidery or lace that makes your gown unique.

Making sure that the bustle is secure is of extreme importance. Ask your dressmaker to show you and the person who will bustle the dress how this is done. You might also ask for spare buttons or hooks. Keep these, plus needle and thread, in your bridal "emergency kit," as they may come in handy if your bustle is too heavy and needs extra support.

The last thing any bride wants is a team of attendants crawling madly around and under her skirt as her anxious guests await her arrival at the reception.

CHAPTER SIXTEEN

WHAT GOES UNDERNEATH:
Your Intimate Apparel

Forget the boob job. Find a bra that fits you perfectly.

One of the most important things to focus on when planning your bridal outfit is making sure that what you wear underneath your wedding dress supports you and the style you are wearing. Different styles need different types of bras to best complement your dress while making your bosom look great. For example, wearing a normal belt bra under a strapless gown would be a mismatch, so here are different types of bras to wear with different silhouettes:

Adhesive bra: Usually intended for halter or backless dresses, as these stick to the bust without straps and hook support. These usually come in two types: paper disposable bras that use a strong adhesive, or bras made of silicone.

Minimizer bra: Commonly sought-after by large-breasted women who wish to reduce the volume of their breasts by a cup or two.

Push-up bra/Maximizer: Ideal for small-chested women who wish to enhance their cleavage, especially on dresses with low necklines. These styles usually have padding or foam inside the padding to help lift the breasts and usually have front closures to give more cleavage.

Corset: Ah, the wonder of the corset! It creates a waist where there is none. This is the most popular bridal bra and is used with most wedding dress styles. It helps give the bride a good posture and comfort while giving the bust an alluring boost and banishes a pouchy stomach without resorting to a "tummy tuck." The weight of the breasts is carried by the whole corset rather than the bra's shoulder straps and, most importantly, it cinches the waist, giving an hourglass look. Avoid it if you're a C or a D cup, though.

Backless bra: Usually lightweight with no back, these are self-adhesive and self-supporting. Ideal for backless dresses and sheer and low-cut necklines, as well as off-the-shoulder numbers.

Half-cup/Demi-cup bra: This is the type of bra where the cup stops just above the nipple. Ideal for the super-low and wide-open necklines. These are supportive, yet provide maximum exposure of the breasts.

Halter-neck bra: These bras have clasps on the straps that attach at the back of the neck and also around the back. Suitable under dresses with halter necklines.

Strapless bra: Designed for strapless dresses, halter necklines, and dress styles that reveal the shoulders, such as off-the-shoulder dresses.

Full-cup bra: This bra provides full support as it comes with underwired cups and covers most of the breasts. Recommended for those with heavier breasts.

Multiway/Convertible bra: One of the best things about this bra is that it comes with detachable straps that can be arranged according to one's needs. It can be worn in a variety of ways or you can have the shoulder straps completely removed, making it versatile enough to be worn with any style of dress, including halter necklines, low backs, strapless and off-the-shoulder numbers.

U-plunge bra: This deep-plunge bra lifts and shapes and allows for lower and increased cleavage. The shoulder straps are usually set wide apart, making it one of the best bras to enhance your cleavage. Suitable for dresses with a deep décolleté or plunging necklines. Pockets allow you to insert silicone pads for extreme cleavage and convertible straps can be worn as conventionally or in a halter or crisscrossed style.

Built-in bra: Ideal for those who don't wish to deal with layers of clothing. This is a supportive bra sewn into the bodice of your dress, providing support without the need for a separate bra. In many cases, this consists of a horizontal elastic strip, cups, and underwires just like separate bra types.

Padded bra: This bra comes with padding inside the cup linings, adding volume to smaller breasts.

Long-line bra: These are bras that extend from the bustline to the waist or hipline and are made to provide maximum support and great shaping, even for larger sizes. They instantly make you look slimmer while providing great support and are very comfortable so your movements are not restricted. Perfect for strapless dresses and unforgiving clingy sheaths.

As you can see, there are so many variations to choose from. The most important thing is to make sure your bra is the right size for you and fits you well. Your bra should conform to the following basic criteria:

- It feels comfortable.
- It lies flat against your back without riding up or sitting too low.
- The gore, which is the part between the cups, lies against your chest as opposed to floating between the breasts.
- The underwires do not sit on top of breast tissue, nor dig into your skin below your armpits.
- The breast tissue is not spilling out on the sides, which may be an indication that the cup size is too small.
- The cups lie flat against your breasts without gapping at the top or causing spill-over.
- The straps are tight enough to stay on your shoulders but do not dig into the skin.

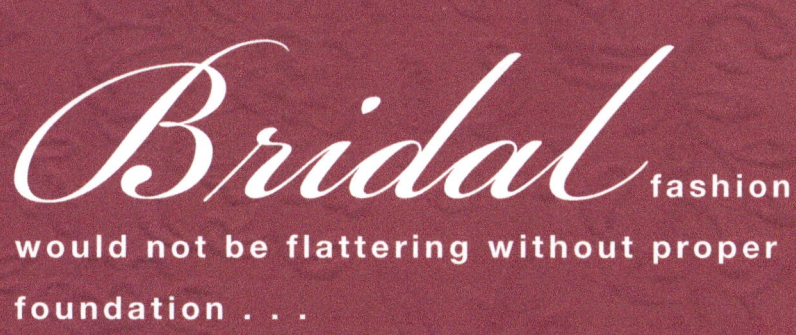

Bridal fashion would not be flattering without proper foundation . . .

Chapter Seventeen

THE PHOTO SHOOT

The camera is a fascinating tool. It can capture that spectacular moment and record it for posterity.

Next to finding your dream dress, styling and planning your bridal photo shoot is one of the most important steps of your wedding. Your photographs document your most important day and freeze your feelings and event to be shared with future generations. Through these photographs, you will be sharing some of the most important and poignant moments of your day.

I love this part of the wedding. Just like a designer runway campaign, deciding the theme and the look of any particular event to ensure that it will accurately portray that most important day is very fulfilling indeed. Go all out for drama and sensuality for your shoot. Your overall look can be inspired by a particular detail of your wedding, perhaps your dress and even the music you have chosen, but most importantly, it captures your feelings and your love for each other.

This is why it is crucial that you interview photographers, check out their wedding portfolios, and pay close attention to how their clients, the brides and grooms, look in the pictures. Were they able to bring out the best in their pictures? Pick a photographer whose work resonates most with what you wish to portray. Consider what style and mood you would like your photographs to convey:

Casual: This is where your photographer captures casual moments during the day and takes candid shots from unconventional angles.

Traditional: These are classic, portrait-style photographs. The pictures are planned carefully and taken in specific poses and lighting.

Artsy: Here the photographer focuses on creating one-of-a-kind photographs capturing you and your party in specific lights and shadows, reminiscent of true art. Often, these are photoshopped and the colors enhanced to inject a dramatic effect.

Choose a photographer who can deliver the style you are looking for. Your photographer is responsible for capturing the light and the essence of every important moment that leads up to your wedding and beyond. Each photographer has their own style and is proficient in delivering certain looks. Therefore, it is quite a chore to interview and screen them, and still make sure your signature look is captured correctly.

Schedule your consultations with your chosen photographer at the venue of your wedding, preferably during the late afternoon, which is generally the time mostly scheduled for photo shoots. Make sure to share how your day's events will unfold and what you are looking for and when and where you would like the pictures taken.

Book your engagement shoots ahead of time, as these can serve as your trials, and determine if the quality you get from your photographer is up to your standards. Find different poses that work best for you—should you look straight at the camera, perhaps tilt your head slightly this way or that? Do you prefer your right side more than the left?

The good news is that you don't have to give up your daily latte to look slimmer in your wedding photos. All you've got to do is position yourself in the most flattering way.

In my St. Pucchi photo shoots, we always use this trick: Place your right foot with toes pointed straight ahead of you, and your left foot behind it at a soft angle, almost forming the letter T. Stand at an angle instead of squaring your body in front of the camera, front hip closest to the camera and the other behind. Keep your shoulders back and natural and stand tall. Your face and shoulders should face the camera. Relax and smile! Once you find which poses flatter you most, stick to those positions for your planned shoot.

The importance of the entire team involved in the shoot is unsurpassable and cannot be discounted. From the makeup artist to the stylist to the hair and nails, everyone has a role to play, each one crucial to the success of your shoot. The flow of the shoot totally depends on the cooperation and harmonious interaction of the crew with one another. Make sure you choose your team wisely.

In preparation for the photo shoot, each minute detail is important, from the appropriate undergarments to the accessories such as shoes and jewelry that will flow well with your dress. Each step can make or break the entire look.

Above all, the backdrop is most crucial. It adds to the atmosphere of the entire shoot. If you are shooting outdoors, then you are dependent on the lighting of the day and must be mindful of the weather on the particular day of the shoot. Make sure the backdrop is not too cluttered and the focus is mostly on you and your party.

Arrange to have access to your wedding venue early so your photographer can take pictures of the wedding décor earlier in the day and before the arrival of your guests. Ideally, the hall you choose should be large, with enough windows to provide natural lighting. This should be where most of your wedding ceremonies are performed to avoid disrupting the effectiveness of the photographer and the hassle of moving your guests from place to place.

Make sure to give your photographer a detailed list of what photos you would like and which moments to capture as they occur, as well as group and family photos and posed ones which are timed. Go over the list thoroughly to avoid any misunderstanding later on.

The following are fourteen handy tips that will help you have that picture-perfect wedding album:

1. Prepare yourself for a long day and be ready to spend hours posing and snapping pictures with those who have gathered to celebrate your day. Don't let frustration seep in and ruin your day.

2. Remember, it is the couple who make the pictures look beautiful. Poses and location are secondary. Plan your own unique pictures; seek inspiration from others, but don't copy.

3. Apply makeup appropriately. The camera picks up details that are sometimes not so visible to the naked eye. Good makeup artists know the tricks required to make you look your best. Test pictures with the actual makeup you will be wearing ahead of time. Beware of ending up looking too orange or yellow, especially if you use bronzer or spray tan.

4. Spare yourself the unnecessary silly gestures and nonsense poses. It may be fun now, but looking back at them in ten and twenty years' time, you may not appreciate them as much.

5. Focus on your posture. No stooping, slouching, shrinking, or being stiff. Keep your shoulders back, pull your stomach in and chest forward. Take frequent

intervals to relax when you're tired, take a deep breath, and pull yourself up again to proceed with the shoot.

6. Know how to pose. For medium-length shots, angle your shoulders toward the camera and then turn your head to look straight at it. This helps smooth out neck wrinkles and makes you look trimmer.

7. When posing in a sleeveless dress, don't press your arms to your sides, as this makes your arms appear larger than they are.

8. Never be photographed holding a drink or a cigarette. The one exception is during the champagne toast (no exceptions for a cigarette!).

9. Ask the photographer to be discreet and capture less obvious but powerful moments such as catching the father seeing his daughter in her dress for the first time or going into the kitchen to shoot whatever's happening there. A unique, telling photo always proves to be a favorite. Discuss ideas with your photographer ahead of time.

10. Try black-and-white film to capture iconic moments such as your walk down the aisle and behind-the-scenes shots as you're getting your makeup done and when you're getting ready.

11. Trust your photographer, follow their directions, and have fun. Leave them to do what they do best and follow their lead on when you should look at the camera and when you shouldn't. Offer suggestions, but don't dictate how your photographer should work. You have chosen them because of their talent and creative genius. Let them do their job and shoot your wedding as they think best.

12. Be your normal self. Don't feel conscious of the camera and let it dictate how you act and behave. Remember, you don't need to smile in all your pictures. Photographs are supposed to capture you in your natural element and not reflect overly exaggerated actions, fake laughter, and very obvious poses.

13. Provide your photographer with a list of everyone you want photographed to avoid disappointment later.

14. Plan your specific group shots early and make sure you don't lose track of the people to be photographed. When you make a list of the must-have group photos, list those who are to be in them. Notify in advance those you'd like to include in portraits. Designate a bridesmaid or groomsman to round up all these people during the photo session so you are not stressed about it.

The entire process can be time-consuming and does not end just with the photo shoot or big event. Pictures are later edited from tens if not hundreds of shots and are photoshopped to remove wrinkles and smeared makeup, etc.

Just enjoy the process.

And don't

forget to

Smile...

not the fake smile,

but one that comes

from deep within.

Chapter Eighteen

THE WEDDING PLANNER

If you're like most brides, by now you're probably overwhelmed! What started off as a beautiful, romantic engagement has now become a frenzy of planning, arranging, and running around to gather the most amazing team that will translate all your wishes into reality.

How can you undertake this huge task and enjoy the process without being stressed out about all the nitty-gritty details? Planning a wedding is a job in and of itself and can take a toll on you while you deal with your everyday life, stress from work, and maintaining a healthy relationship with your loved ones. At times, it may feel like the wedding is consuming every waking hour. You go to bed and wake up thinking of the different tasks that lie ahead, and you find yourself losing your cool more often than not and being burnt out.

While it is in no way impossible to plan your wedding by yourself, a good wedding planner can make your journey less stressful, as they have valuable experience handling weddings and the myriad details and tasks that need to be arranged and coordinating the several people shaping your event.

If budget allows, and you do not have the required time, patience, or organizational skills or the ability to handle the daily stress, then by all means, hire a wedding planner. And if the wedding location is far away from where you live and you cannot effectively monitor everything, then that is all the more reason to have a wedding planner.

Moreover, there are some things that only your wedding planner can do, such as use their contacts to get you to the right and reliable people for each task, advise you on what is possible and what is not, handle any emergency or sticky situation that calls for attention, and have a plan B in place. Most of all, having a planner gives you the peace of mind and the freedom to enjoy yourself without feeling stressed out.

You will thank yourself for your decision to hire a wedding planner and find that it may be the best investment you made. Planning a wedding should be fun, not stressful. You can now relax and focus on being happily engaged while looking forward to a memorable wedding day with excitement and anticipation, knowing that some professional, responsible being is helping you tackle every wedding task and has your best interests at heart.

Depending on your budget, you have a choice of either hiring a full-service professional wedding planner to handle *all* the details of your wedding or one who will help you with partial services.

How do you find the right wedding planner to whom you can delegate such a huge responsibility and trust will come through for you?

What exactly does a wedding planner do, anyway? Here are your answers . . .

A FULL-SERVICE EVENT PLANNER

This is someone who will take care of all tasks, be involved in every aspect of planning your wedding, and be responsible for executing everything at your wedding to ensure everything goes smoothly. Some of the tasks include but are not limited to:

- Customize your wedding checklist and create a schedule with specific timelines for the completion of every task
- Interview, select, and book vendors who will handle each aspect of the wedding
- Negotiate, discuss, and coordinate tasks with each vendor
- Hire the venue
- Book florists, caterers, the band, etc.
- Plan each and every fine detail of the wedding from décor to table settings, party favors, flowers, cake, photography, music, etc.
- Create invitations
- Send thank-you notes
- Coordinate and help with your dress purchase, fittings, and delivery
- Guide you on wedding etiquette
- Plan and prepare for the day and foresee possible pitfalls
- Take care of all after-the-wedding tasks (see Chapter 23: Marriage Legalities)

PART-TIME WEDDING PLANNER

Rather than outsourcing the entire wedding planning process, hire a part-time planner to help with selected aspects that you find too time-consuming or challenging to handle by yourself. Part-time planners generally charge a flat fee for the service(s) delegated to them and are more budget-friendly. They can help you perform chosen tasks, some of which may include the following:

- Suggest décor
- Assist in finding and booking vendors
- Take charge of all details on your wedding day

DAY-OF-WEDDING COORDINATOR

I highly recommend you at least consider hiring a wedding planner for the day of the wedding. So many things need your attention on that day, and things can go awry when you least expect them to. Besides, you want to have a stress-free wedding day instead of worrying about last-minute details. Even if you have handled everything about your wedding up to this point, your coordinator is there to help make sure everything progresses smoothly as per your plan, including but not limited to making sure your bridesmaids know when to be where, that the venue is arranged just like you want it, that guests are comfortably seated, vendors deliver on time, food and drinks are served at the right time, cake is sliced and served properly, music is played when it should be, etc.

Do your homework and prepare a shortlist of professionals who are experienced and well trained and check their references before conducting interviews to zero in on your choice. At the interview, ask lots of questions: How do they work? What will be their contribution to your wedding? How do they find, hire, and manage their support team? How do they handle emergencies and last-minute changes?

As you communicate with them, pay attention to how you feel: Are you comfortable discussing your ideas? Do they welcome your ideas and build on them? Is there a rapport between you right from the start? If you feel you are struggling to convince them of what it is you want, and they seem set in their ways, then obviously they are not the right choice.

Discuss the cost and what will be included, and make sure all the terms and conditions are spelled out very clearly and included in the final contract. The planning process begins as soon as you have finalized the contract, so be in touch and have regular meetings to go over and get updates on the progress periodically. From the minute your wedding planner is assigned responsibility, they start working toward making your wedding a success. It is a service you are paying for that must be delivered to your satisfaction.

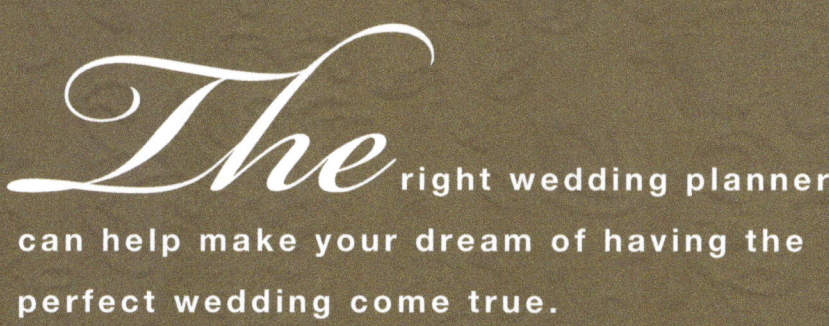

The right wedding planner can help make your dream of having the perfect wedding come true.

Chapter Nineteen

BRIDESMAIDS:
Yes or No?

"**G**ain a husband, lose a friend?"

Weddings can be quite stressful, especially when you are the bride and your intention is to maintain peace among friends.

In my years of working with brides I have seen more petty disputes among brides and the women chosen as their bridesmaids than I can recall. Mid-planning, I have seen some bridesmaids vanish only to be replaced by other friends at the last minute. And a third of these relationships fall out after the wedding day due to jealousy and resentment taking friendships to a breaking point.

So, what can you as the bride do to keep the peace? Here are six tips:

1. Be sure that you pick and choose your bridesmaids well. These would be the women you are closest to and trust the most, those you feel are responsible and care enough to stand by you and help see you through your crazy wedding planning days.

2. Be considerate and sensitive to their feelings, and involve and engage with them rather than think only about yourself. After all, your maids have in essence agreed to be fully on board while accepting the title, and any distress over your decisions can create a rift in an otherwise great friendship.

3. Be reasonable when setting a budget for their dress unless you are footing the bill. Discuss and consult with them on what they can afford and fix a budget that is within their means. A new dress, accessories, and shoes can add up quickly and cause hardship and create undue stress.

4. Choose a style that is classic and not too "bridesmaid"-looking so they can wear it again. One idea is to choose a color that everyone will wear, but allow them to pick their own style that flatters their figure best and makes them feel special.

5. Be appreciative of whatever they plan for your celebrations such as your bridal shower and bachelorette party. Paying for their attire is already a stretch for many, so do not expect them to spend more than they can afford on parties.

6. Be grateful. Your bridesmaids are your friends who have devoted their time and energy to see your wedding plans through with you, so thank them like you mean it. Gift them with something special. It could even be the jewelry they will wear on the day or a gift basket to indulge in. Write them a thank-you note and let them know how much they mean to you.

Some brides today opt not to have bridesmaids at their wedding. This is really a personal choice.

If choosing friends to don matching dresses and stand beside you on your big day doesn't feel right, then you don't have to have bridesmaids. Your friends can be your guests instead of maids and actually have fun at your wedding. The "traditional" bridal rules no longer exist. Besides, you may have a variety of reasons, all valid, such as:

- You have too many family members and friends and don't want to upset any of them. It can be tricky to choose and keep the peace.
- You wish to save everyone some serious cash, seeing how much it costs to get a dress and accessories, travel, reserve accommodations, purchase gifts, and contribute toward a bachelorette party. Besides, you, as the bride, have to spend on gifts, meals, transportation, and hair and makeup. When all is said and done, skipping the maids is not a bad idea if you're planning your wedding on a tight budget.
- You'd rather not have to deal with the added stress and drama, which can surely happen even among the best of friends.
- You would rather have the wedding be all about you as a couple.
- You're planning a small and casual or intimate wedding without the traditional implications and are trying to keep things seriously low-key.

True friends will understand that their presence is meaningful enough.

Whatever your decision in this matter, remember that your wedding day is a celebration, not a cause for any undue stress.

Chapter Twenty

MOTHER OF THE BRIDE

Watching your daughter tie the knot can be the most poignant and exciting moment of your life, so it is quite normal to feel overwhelmed.

Naturally, you want to look amazing at this memorable event, without compromising on your own style personality. The memories of that day will be captured in photos and you will want to look your best.

Here are some tips and rules to follow:

Pick a color that suits you most: As we age, our skin loses a little rosiness, so be mindful not to choose a color that will wash you out. Your hair and eye color as well as your skin tone are also determining factors. The color of your dress must not be the same as your daughter's wedding dress—nor all black. And it certainly must not match what the bridesmaids are wearing.

Avoid flashy shades like extremely bright red, pink, or yellow, as the dress may stand out too much. Best to stay with subtler colors or a multicolored dress that mixes subtlety with brightness, which comes across as more elegant.

Most importantly, the color of your dress should be unique to your personality while also in keeping with the color scheme of the wedding.

Wear a silhouette that flatters your body type: I express very clearly how you can determine your body type and what suits you best in my book *Your Body, Your Style: Simple Tips on Dressing to Flatter Your Body Type*. Feel free to go through it to help you make the right decision.

Whatever you wear, make sure it's not overly sexy. Avoid too much cleavage and let the bride be the sexiest girl in the room.

Wear the right undergarments: There is a lot of help out there as far as support garments and modern-day girdles. The right bra and lingerie can not only contribute to a better-fitting garment but also boost your confidence.

Invest in your hair and makeup: Get your hair done professionally. A fresh color and blowout goes a long way. Your makeup, too, must be such that it highlights your best features. You will be in the spotlight and in many photographs on the big day, so definitely go for a little definition around the eyes, fill in your eyebrows, wear soft-colored eyeshadow and mascara to open up your eyes, and wear a deeper color on your lips and contoured cheekbones if necessary. A professional makeup artist is highly recommended.

Above all, smile!

Your attitude is a reflection of the

joy you feel inside,

and others can sense that.

Smile,
Relax,
and
have fun!

CHAPTER TWENTY-ONE

GETTING IN SHAPE FOR YOUR WEDDING DAY

One of the biggest concerns brides have is shedding some weight and looking great in their wedding dress.

Losing weight, especially at a time when you are stressed about your wedding, is not easy. Your diet and eating patterns need to change long before your big day, not just during the last few days or weeks. Yo-yo diets never work in the long run, so what you really want to do is change your eating habits early on so you can keep the weight off, be toned, and also increase your energy level long after the wedding is over.

Here are some things you can introduce into your daily lifestyle, perhaps starting as early as the day you pin down your wedding date, and certainly at least six months prior to the big day.

DETOX

Why? Because a proper detox will clean your system from the inside out. It will clear your mind, body, and spirit and help you become more mindful of what you put into your body while inspiring you toward better eating habits. Detox also helps skin, hair, and nails, prevents bloating, and boosts your energy level as well as helping get your body on track with better sleeping patterns.

Some cleansing programs include colon hydrotherapy, juice fasts, and exercise and meditation, all of which help balance your body and mind. Note: A juice cleanse lasting for more than five days should only be done under controlled conditions like in a detox spa.

EAT HEALTHY

The most important thing is to make sure you are eating the right types of food to stay healthy. Combining the right types of foods helps support the liver, eliminate belly bloat, and contribute to natural weight loss. Keep your body alkaline.

Making your body alkaline is easy. Here are some simple rules to follow to alkalize your body for more energy and vitality:

- Start your day with the juice of one lemon in warm water.
- Eat a large green salad tossed in lemon juice and olive oil.
- Snack on raw, unsalted almonds.
- Drink a non-dairy milk or berry smoothie with added green powder like spirulina, chlorella, or other greens.
- Skip the sugar-laden dessert or soda.
- Stick to a plant-based diet.

Eat fruit by itself on an empty stomach, preferably first thing in the morning; eat proteins with vegetables; eat carbs and starchy foods by themselves or with a vegetable; and drink eight glasses of water per day.

Introduce the following into your daily diet: lots of vegetables, fish, lean chicken, and a little fruit. Substitute one meal for a liquid meal instead. Add barley, greens, or spirulina powders to juices to help curb your appetite and hunger pangs. Stay away from prepackaged juices, which are loaded with sugar. Juice must be made fresh and consumed instantly for maximum benefit. Some ingredients to consider for juicing are apples and cucumber, which are great for flushing out the system; celery, to help reduce acidity; ginger, which is a natural antibiotic; and lemon, to help remove harmful bacteria and toxins from the intestinal tract and clear the liver and kidneys.

Cut out for at least a few weeks prior to your wedding day things such as sugar, alcohol, soda, caffeine, refined carbs, saturated fats found in cheeses and heavy meats, and fried foods from your diet.

EXERCISE

Make some time each day to exercise. Working up a good sweat can easily turn your day around and release endorphins, giving you the post-workout bliss so many talk about. Your exercise routine can be as simple as a brisk walk, jogging around the block, or even dancing to your favorite music. Moving your body not only helps eliminate stress and clear your mind, but also gets you in shape quickly. Moreover, exercise helps move acidic waste products so your body can better eliminate them.

Developing a regular exercise routine can also become part of a special bonding ritual when undertaken with your fiancé or even your bridesmaids. You could meet up at a gym or even at a park regularly to enjoy a little time away from the wedding planning process, relax, and enjoy each other's company.

SLEEP WELL

Commit to getting at least seven to eight hours of sleep each night. Lack of sleep is not only detrimental to your health, but also one of the main causes of weight gain.

Recent studies have suggested an association between sleep duration and weight fluctuation. One explanation is that sleep duration affects hormones regulating hunger—ghrelin and leptin—and stimulates the appetite. Loss of sleep tends to lead to sugar and fat cravings as well as reduced willpower. The researchers hypothesize that shorter sleepers may actually have slower metabolisms and that people sleeping in the seven-to-nine-hour range are less likely to be overweight than those who sleep less.

To help you sleep better, keep all technology out of the bedroom. Turn off all your devices at least thirty minutes prior to bedtime and escort them outside of your bedroom. Spend the last half-hour reading something not related to your work, or better still, write in a gratitude journal or meditate.

Getting your fill of sleep will make you feel refreshed and ready to take on whatever each day may bring.

Whatever

you do, keep your goals realistic and

celebrate any progress made along the way.

By the time your wedding day arrives,

you will not only feel relaxed

—you will feel great.

Chapter Twenty-Two

WEDDING DAY MISHAPS

Although you spend countless hours planning and making sure everything will go perfectly, unpleasant surprises may come up when you least expect them.

If caught in the midst of a wedding day disaster, take a deep breath and try out these tips. Although they probably won't be enough to fix a major snafu, they will likely solve most of the issues:

You wake up on the day of your wedding to red, splotchy skin or a giant zit: Reach out to a dermatologist for help in minimizing inflammation as soon as possible. If that's not an option, then work with concealers and foundation to get the most natural-looking coverage.

A vendor cancels on you at the last minute: Recruit the help of your other vendors or ask recently married friends or relatives to see if they know anyone who can fill the role at the last minute.

The zipper on your gown breaks, or worse still, your gown rips: Unfortunately, wedding day dress disasters are more common than not. One can never predict what may happen with something as delicate as a wedding dress with its delicate details and expensive fabrics. Stains, tears, and even broken zippers are every bride's nightmare. The best thing you can do is to prepare for the worst-case scenario by keeping the following things handy and making sure you have someone who can step in and help do damage control. Your emergency bridal kit should include the following:

- Safety pins
- Fabric glue
- Extra buttons
- Sewing kit with needles and threads
- Stain remover
- Transparent tape
- Talcum powder
- Cotton swabs
- White chalk
- Tissues
- Moist wipes

Seek help from your wedding planner or someone in your bridal party who knows their way with a needle and thread to do damage control. Tackle tears promptly to prevent the existing rip from becoming any bigger. If the patch shows, try to camouflage the spot by holding your bridal bouquet over it or covering it with your veil.

The weather turns suddenly and it pours: Either move your activities indoors if possible, or find a rental company who can install a tent on short notice.

The car breaks down: Make sure your transportation company is a dependable one and has a replacement available immediately. Barring that, seek the help of a friend or relative to drive you so you will arrive on time.

The cake is ruined during delivery: If your baker has backup baked goods, then great, but if not, you could camouflage the damaged areas with flowers or other decorations and turn the spotlight away from the cake.

You spill food or red wine on your dress: Tend to this immediately before the stain settles. Make sure to use the right stain remover for your fabric, or you may end up doing more damage. Dab the area with a white piece of cloth. Begin at the outside and work your way toward the middle of the stain. Next, apply a small amount of club soda to the stain and continue to dab it until the stain is removed. Finally, use a blow-dryer set on low to dry the spot. If signs of the stain still remain, use white chalk or talcum powder to cover it up. White chalk or powder over the colored area will help make it not so obvious. If you notice an oil mark, quickly dust it with talcum powder, let it soak up the oil, and then dust it off.

Tripping over your dress: Make sure your wedding dress hemline is correct by trying it on with your wedding shoes to make sure you can walk comfortably and elegantly without tripping. Have your seamstress lift the hem on the center front by one inch shorter than the sides to eliminate this potential problem. It takes just a little extra length for you to trip over your dress, so practice walking in your gown and climbing stairs before you wear it on your wedding day.

Slipping on the carpet: This usually happens if the soles of your new leather shoes are too smooth. Rub the bottoms of leather shoes with sandpaper or stick cute sandpaper hearts on the soles to give them a grip and make them less slippery.

While some big things could go wrong on your wedding day, remember, your attitude matters. Laughter, not tears, will make your day that much more memorable and unique.

CHAPTER TWENTY-THREE

MARRIAGE LEGALITIES

Many starry-eyed couples think of marriage as a simple, romantic ceremony that binds them for life, yet few truly understand the complex legalities of marriage. Too many issues come into play, and it is important to understand some of these before you embark on your journey.

Getting married involves legal expenses, ramifications, and requirements. Below is a guide to some legal practicalities that need to be in place:

Marriage license: Obviously, you cannot get married without a license. You must apply for your license at the county clerk's office. Make sure to check your county's exact requirements for documents they may need and take them along with you. These may include at least one form of ID, proof of divorce or death of a spouse in the case of a previous marriage, and medical test results.

You must have your license with you on your wedding day. After the ceremony is over, it is your officiant's responsibility to return it to the authorities to process so you may receive your marriage certificate.

If you're getting married abroad, confirm that the marriage certificate you will receive will satisfy the requirements of your state. The best way to ensure that your foreign marriage is recognized in the United States is to go to the United States Embassy or Consulate in that country to have them authenticate foreign marriage documents. The rules permitting you to prove the validity of your marriage abroad vary greatly depending upon the country where you are married or the United States' acceptance of that country's recording system. To avoid many potential headaches and expenditures, you could ask your officiant to issue your marriage license and officiate your private ceremony in the United States either before or after your foreign marriage ceremony. To be absolutely sure, do check all the legalities before you make your final plans.

Joint taxes, debts, and liabilities: As a couple, you will have a choice of either filing joint taxes or continuing to file separately. Whether you are responsible for your partner's debts when you marry depends on the state you live in. In community property states, all debts incurred by either of you during the marriage (not before) will be owed by both of you regardless.

Prenuptial agreement: When one is in love, tending fences can be overlooked. However, since so many marriages end in separation or divorce today, having a prenuptial agreement in place is wise. Having a prenup doesn't mean that your marriage will fail or that you don't love each other. It just helps each partner keep what was originally his or hers in individual, separate accounts. This saves you from being embroiled in any lawsuits or held accountable for your spouse's previous debts so that you don't risk having to split your premarital assets in a divorce. Consult with your lawyer and make sure your prenup is watertight and spans the length of your marriage. Both sides must have legal representation for a prenup to be valid.

Changing your name: Of the various options you have to change your name, which one would you want to reflect your new identity after marriage? You can either keep the one you have now, take a hyphenated name, or combine your names into one new one to use as a couple. Determine what feels right to you and what is important to both of you. If you decide to change your name, you will need to fill in your new name on your marriage license on the day of your wedding so that your marriage certificate reflects your new name. Next, you will need to change your name on all official documents starting with your social security card.

Start with this name change checklist:

- __ Social security card (do this first)
- __ Driver's license (do this second)
- __ Vehicle registration
- __ Car title
- __ Mortgage/Rent
- __ Debit/Credit cards
- __ Checks
- __ Passport
- __ Insurance (home, auto, life, flood, etc.)
- __ Doctor's office, dentist's office
- __ Personal email/Personal email signature
- __ Social media
- __ Voicemail greetings

__ Business cards
__ Human resources
__ Professional organizations
__ W2 forms

Adding/changing beneficiary information: This pertains to your insurance policies. Remember to change/add your beneficiary on your life insurance and any other insurance policies you may have.

Wills: Ask your lawyer for legal advice, especially if you have complex assets and arrangements. Note: You'll automatically be considered next of kin once you're married, and any decisions (such as medical) may be deferred directly to you by default.

No Matter

how long you've been married or

whether you are newly engaged,

it is important to understand

the legalities of marriage to

protect your rights.

Chapter Twenty-Four

AFTER THE WEDDING

You are finally a "Mrs." and probably relieved after the whirlwind of activities around the wedding planning. You can finally step back, relax, and settle into your new life. The wedding day flew by like a dream and just a few final tasks remain that need your attention.

Here are some of them:

___*Sort your gifts and send thank-you notes:* Prepare a list of the gifts as they are received/opened and note details such as what the gift was and who sent it. This will allow you to prepare your thank-you notes faster. Make sure to have your stationary ready and your notes mailed within a month of your wedding. Your guests will feel better appreciated if you send hand-written thank-you notes than if you send them a printed one.

___*Get your name changed:* Only if you have decided to do so. Of the various options you have, which name would you want to reflect your new identity after marriage? You can either keep the one you have now, take a hyphenated name, or combine your names into one new one to use as a couple. Determine what feels right for you and is important to both of you. If you do decide to change your name, then you will need to collect your marriage license and visit the appropriate government agencies, banks, and medical and financial institutions to update your records with your new name. Ditto for your insurance plans and beneficiary updates. (See the name change checklist in Chapter 23: Marriage Legalities.)

___*Get your dress cleaned as soon as possible:*** Stains and dirt from the wedding day can set in quickly and become difficult to remove, so make sure you send your gown to a reputable and professional cleaning company that specializes in bridal gowns as soon as the wedding is over. Note: If you're planning on heading directly from your wedding to your honeymoon, ask someone to prepare your gown for storage and either ship or drop it off to the cleaners as soon as possible since some stains, like red wine, can set permanently.

___*Preserve your dress:*** Your wedding gown is a treasure trove of memories and you will want to preserve it for posterity. Years from now you'll be able to take it out without fear of discovering stains or fade spots. Perhaps you can even pass it on to your daughter for her wedding.

Although packaging heirloom dresses can be done at home, it is best you leave that task to the professionals and have it packaged commercially. Preservation companies know how to go through the various sensitive steps to ensure your gown will endure time and check carefully for soils and stains as well as remove any wrinkles that may have been pressed in. Fabric-covered metal buttons, foam padding, and rubberized dress shields can oxidize, rust, or deteriorate over time and damage the fabric of your wedding gown. Moreover, packing and storing to preserve a gown is complicated and best left to the experts.

Once your gown is cleaned, preserved, and boxed professionally, simply store the box away. Peek in on your gown a couple of times a year to make sure there's no discoloration, mildew, or pest infestation. If you do find a problem, contact your dry cleaner and preservation company for advice.

OTHER COOL OPTIONS FOR YOUR GOWN . . .

How else can you preserve your precious wedding gown? You have probably spent days or even months searching for the prefect wedding dress, but as soon as the wedding is over, it gets put in a box and packed away. This seems completely ridiculous to me, especially since you likely spent an arm and a leg on the dress. But, what other options do you have?

Take a cue from one of the Real Housewives of Beverly Hills, Adrienne Maloof, who had her St. Pucchi wedding dress vacuum-sealed and displayed it in a tall glass case in a focal point of a room.

Consider framing yours and showcasing it in a large walk-in closet or display it on a mannequin . . .

Your wedding gown deserves the best room in the house.

Chapter Twenty-Five

FAQ:
53 OF YOUR MOST PRESSING QUESTIONS ANSWERED

Below is a list of the most common questions and concerns asked by brides from across the globe. Here are my thoughts . . .

1. How soon should I announce my engagement on social media?

The most important family members and friends should be informed before the rest of the world finds out. People can be sensitive, especially if they find out secondhand about your big decision. This way, you're showing them how much you care. The days when everyone else discovered your big news via the announcement section in the Sunday edition of the local paper are behind us. Social media is the new platform. Ring selfies and hashtags perfectly communicate your new relationship status. Make sure to include your significant other when sharing your joy. Take the time to look your best for the pictures, and even borrow (and credit) someone else's timeless words when posting.

2. I don't know where to start to plan for my wedding. Do you recommend that I go to a bridal show before all else?

A bridal show is a great place to gather some ideas for your wedding, but it can be overwhelming with so many products on display and vendors clamoring for your attention. Take a file folder with you so you can be organized as you gather pamphlets and information to browse through for later. Be prepared and don't be shy about asking vendors important questions such as how long they've been in business, how many weddings they take on in a year, their references, previous reviews and testimonials, contact information, pricing packages, and most importantly, whether they have all the necessary certifications. If you're pleased with what they offer, ask to set up a meeting to discuss the details of your wedding. There is no need to make any firm decisions at the show. Remember, you're there only to gather information.

3. How should I decide whether to go for strapless or opt for straps on my wedding dress?

If you are a little more on the busty side, you may opt for straps to hold you in place. Also, if your dress has a very low backline, having a strap will ensure that the dress is snug on your body. Straps provide you with confidence and keep you from constantly wanting to pull up your bodice.

4. I am a full-figured bride, and most salons I've visited do not carry designer gowns in my size for me to try on. The ones they do carry in my size are by low-budget designers. Any suggestions?

Your best bet would be to shop at a salon that specializes in plus sizes. However, if they, too, do not carry the designer you are drawn to, then your only other option would be to improvise. Most wedding dress designers and manufacturers do produce their designs in plus sizes, although because of the extra costs for larger-size samples, many stores do not stock samples in sizes above 12 or 14. Be assured that most bridal stores are able to help you get a fairly good idea of how a certain dress will look on you by working with clamps and modesty pieces during your try-on.

5. I intend to lose quite a bit of weight before my wedding. Should I order my gown in a smaller size?

It's probably not a good idea. Most brides I have worked with come to us with this expectation. While it's commendable, I have noticed more often than not, with all the tension that goes with the planning of a wedding, the added pressure of losing weight can be almost unbearable, making it harder to reach weight loss goals. Note that it is always better to order the dress in your current size and have it taken in during the fitting process than to order a smaller size, not meet your weight loss goal, and be miserable because you cannot fit into it. Remember, not too much can be done to make a smaller gown larger.

6. Is it okay to request children not be present at my wedding?

This is a personal choice. Many couples choose not to invite children, while others look forward to not only having them there but also including them in the ceremony as either flower girls, ring-bearers, or train-bearers. While you can expect older children to behave, you may have to be prepared for last-minute tantrums and tears with the younger children. Talk to the parents and find out how you can help make their children comfortable. With a little luck and planning, everything should go smoothly and the children will remember you fondly for including them and even honoring them with a role at your wedding or just as a guest at the grandest party of their lives (so far).

7. How much should my fiancé be involved in the wedding planning?

While the groom has been generally expected to play a supporting role, there's a growing trend that today's grooms help plan the wedding. Grooms now are apt to be older and more established and so may be paying much of the expenses along with the brides. One of the areas where I have seen their involvement in is money matters and budgeting. In this area, when a woman becomes a bride, cutting down costs becomes an alien concept. So, having him involved is not necessarily a bad thing, especially when planning the venue location, guest list, wedding music, his tux, and even the wedding registry.

Share your plans and progress with your fiancé every now and then. Discuss with him your concerns and worries and let him have a say. He may have not the slightest clue as to what you are talking about when you communicate your ideas about the invitations, flowers, your dilemma when deciding between lilac and blush for your wedding palette, your wedding dress and jewelry, etc., but that doesn't matter. There are plenty of duties to share—including writing all the thank-you notes! As long as you make him feel he is part of the process, it will make him feel good. Take time out from your wedding planning once in a while, rather than spend all your time together talking about the wedding. Remember not to lose sight of the fact that the main reason you are tying the knot together is to celebrate your love for each other.

8. Any suggestions for arriving in style and making the perfect entrance to my wedding?

With so many things on your plate and the pressure to make sure everything is taken care of in a timely fashion, certain aspects such as transportation to the wedding take the backseat. Getting to the wedding on time and finding a balance between reliable, affordable, practical transportation and a unique, memorable method of arriving in style is a challenge for most brides. Here are a few ideas:

Limousine or car: A limousine will give you the extra room to make sure your gown is not wrinkled by the time you get to your destination. What is the theme of your wedding? If it's traditional, then a classic car or a stretch limousine is perfect. If it's vintage-inspired then how about an old Volkswagen beetle or a retro camper van? To add a touch of style, you could go for a sports car like a Lamborghini Gallardo. Classic cars such as the Rolls Royce and Bentley work with any theme.

Horse and carriage: In true fairy-tale fashion, the horse and carriage is another classy way of arriving at your venue. However, this mode of transportation is very weather-dependent so make sure it works for the time of the year, or else opt for a carriage with an extendable roof.

By sea: A boat is ideal for a beach wedding. It would be such a shame not to make the most of the stunning scenery by arriving on a luxury yacht or a speedboat. An old-fashioned gondola is also very elegant and romantic.

By air: For the ultra-adventurous, how about a hot air balloon? Or perhaps go all-out glam by arriving in your very own chartered helicopter. This would be especially impressive if you are having an outdoor wedding, either on a sprawling estate or a hilltop venue. Your guests could even watch you exit while toasting your marriage as you sail through the sky in your hot air balloon.

9. How do I manage my dress while getting in and out of my limousine?

If you are wearing a ball gown or a full-skirted dress: Pick it up gently from the hem and lift the skirt up so you're not sitting on it and causing it to crease. You should be sitting on your slip or petticoat and not on the actual dress. Spread the skirt out on the seat as much as possible. When you exit, pick the dress up again from the bottom and carefully step out.

If your dress has a detachable train: Make sure to keep the train aside and only put it on when you get to the venue.

If your dress has a narrow skirt: Slide into the car and sit at an angle rather than upright, so you don't crease the middle of the dress, keeping your legs as straight as possible.

10. Is a wedding registry a good idea? How do I tell guests about it without coming across as "asking?"

While some couples feel wedding registries are not such a good idea because it gives the impression that you are fishing for gifts, it certainly helps guests find useful gifts specifically picked by you rather than having to find random items that may not be to your liking. In essence, you are making their lives easier, especially for those guests who have no idea of your tastes and what would be actually useful to you. If you feel uncomfortable telling your guests where you are registered, you can entrust this task to your mother or members of your wedding party so they can pass the information along.

Consider the following approaches:

- Plan your list sensibly when registering for gifts. Think of your potential long-term needs and which gifts will last and serve you best.
- Register for a variety of gifts in different price ranges to give your guests enough choices based on their budget.
- Take time to research your options and register at few select stores only, particularly ones that allow guests to purchase online to make it convenient for them. Also look into shipping and delivery options, exchange and return policies, and any discounts or offers that you can take advantage of.

11. When is it best to have a bridal Shower and what is the etiquette around this?

Two to six months before the wedding is the ideal time, as you don't want it too close to your wedding date. Best to space out the events to avoid overwhelming your guests. This is a great opportunity to socialize with friends and family and an excuse for your guests to shower you with gifts (hence the term "bridal shower"). There are no rules as to who should host the shower, as more and more mothers and sisters are acting as hostesses nowadays. A relative may offer to throw you the shower, or a friend may offer to host a more laid-back bash where you can invite your pals. It's totally cool to have multiple showers.

12. Is it necessary to hire a makeup artist if I can do my own makeup?

Your makeup artist is just as important as your hairstylist. You may think you are great at doing your own makeup, but trust me when I say this is a worthwhile investment. There is a vast difference between everyday makeup versus makeup for your special day. Consider that you will be on center stage and lights and cameras are on you. The proper makeup will make you glow and cover any imperfections that cameras tend to capture. As with all other vendors and service providers, you must do your research and have a trial makeup session. Gather ideas and photos to show your makeup artist the kind of makeup you're looking for so she can try it on you to see how you like it and adjust it to your liking. This is a perfect time to make sure your skin is not sensitive to the products that will be used. Don't skip the makeup trial, as your face will thank you for it and there will be no last-minute surprises and upsets.

13. Are there specific rules for wedding invitations?

Many of the exact same rules of yesteryear apply today when it comes to wedding invitation etiquette. Invitations aren't just about picking the perfect paper, colors, or designs, but are also a reflection of your unique style and personality while providing your guests with the details of your highly anticipated event.

The main rule to follow is to always include the three W's:

WHO—full name of bride and groom

WHEN—date, time, month, and year

WHERE—the location of your wedding, complete with the full address of the venue (you can either include the reception information or opt to print a separate invite for it)

Decide whether you would like to use formal or casual phrasing on your invitations. Formal phrasing works for any type of wedding and is especially appropriate for a church ceremony. A formal invitation is where the dates and times are spelled out rather than abbreviated and may look like this:

Mr. & Mrs. John Wyatt
Request the Pleasure of Your Company
at the Marriage of Their Daughter
Holly Wyatt
to
David Smith
Saturday, the Ninth of September
Two Thousand and Eighteen
Four O'Clock in the Afternoon
Churchill Manor
485 Brown Street
Napa, California
Reception to Follow

A casual invitation may have a more artistic, whimsical feel to it, where you can loosen up the language and use actual numbers instead of spelling them out. It is absolutely acceptable if you're having a laid-back wedding. You can even opt to replace the hosts' names with something simpler such as, "Together with their families . . ." To avoid confusion, you can look at examples of other wedding invitations for inspiration.

Do not include your gift or registry information on the actual invite, but have separate cards with the information instead. Do include reception RSVP cards in the same envelope as your wedding invitations.

14. How can I make an elegant walk down the aisle?

Walking down the aisle is perhaps the most important part of the ceremony. All eyes are on you, so it is important that you get this part right. Practice the walk before the actual day; you will be calmer and more at ease during the ceremony. Smile as you walk and show your guests how happy you are. Don't just stare ahead—notice the friendly faces, and with a soft smile, show your guests how much you appreciate them being there.

Walk as you normally do, just a little slower. Keep your shoulders back, but don't look stiff. The key word is pacing—keep pace with the processional music. Practice the slow walk to music at home to become familiar with the beat. The whole reason that step-tap-step-tap gait originated is because it forces you to slow down.

Your escort needs to lock arms with you, not the other way around. Only then can you hold your bouquet in the right position, which is lower than you think. Creating a diamond shape between the arms and body, hold the bouquet closer to your hips than to your chest.

15. I'm confused about the wedding perfume to choose. What are your suggestions?

Depends on the season you're getting married in. I recommend floral fragrances for summer weddings and warm scents for winter weddings. Your perfume should not clash with your groom's, so make sure to pick a scent that works in tandem and not against each other. Nor should it clash with your bouquet, especially if it is formed of natural flowers that will have a strong scent already. Smells create very vivid memories, so make sure to take your time when choosing your perfume. It's best to go perfume shopping during the afternoon, when your sense of smell works best. Try on the ones you like best (no more than two at a time or it can cause sensory overload), by spraying at different locations. The smell takes time to settle, so you should wait at least a couple of hours, or make another trip, before deciding on the one. However, if you already have a perfume that you love and have worn forever, stick with it. Some things are best left unchanged. (I have written extensively on this subject and how to wear your perfume in the chapter "Scent of a Woman" in my book *Your Body, Your Style: Simple Tips on Dressing to Flatter Your Body Type.)*

16. I lost my father and wish he could see me walk down the aisle. Any advice on how I can include him in some way on my big day?

While nothing can replace a loved one's presence at your wedding, there are a few beautiful ways to include them in your most important day. Here are a few:

Incorporate a piece of their clothing: For our bride Elizabeth, we took the monogrammed cuffs of her father's blue shirt and embroidered them into a heart-shaped piece which was sewn into the side seam of her bodice. This also gave her the "something blue" to wear.

Save them a seat: Some brides leave an empty chair at the ceremony or reception, placing a flower or even their picture on the seat, as a tribute to their loved one.

Wear a piece of their jewelry: A piece of jewelry, particularly something sentimental like their brooch, hair-pin, or earrings, is sure to make you feel their presence and at the same time doubles up as your "something old" and "something borrowed."

Dedicate a song or a poem to them: Your loved one's favorite song or a poem can be a part of the ceremony and allows you to honor your loved ones.

17. I'm considering having a destination wedding overseas. How can I transport my dress so it arrives safely?

If your wedding dress is bulky, then it's best to ship it ahead of time. Call your hotel and ask to speak to the manager to make sure they will hold your shipment in a safe spot until you arrive.

Crowded airports, weather delays, clogged freeways—all are super-stressful, but lost luggage is quite possibly the worst offender. One way to ensure you dress makes it to your destination? Hand-carry it onto the flight, but make sure to check with your airline in advance to see if they would be willing to store it in the first-class cabin wardrobe. If not, then pack it in a maximum-size-allowed hard-sided carry-on cabin suitcase. Whatever you do, do not check it in with your luggage. Airlines are notorious for losing luggage, and this is one that needs to be watched closely.

18. What is the correct and the easiest way to get into my gown?

Get your hair and makeup done (everything but your lipstick, that is) before putting on your gown or else you risk wrinkling the fabric and getting makeup on it. Place a sheet on the floor, hold your gown over it then step into the dress. If your gown calls for a slip, other than the one already built in the dress, then put the slip inside the dress and step into both at the same time. You will need someone to hold the waist open while you get into the dress.

19. I'm wearing a big ball gown for my wedding and I'm concerned about having to use the bathroom. How am I supposed to manage my dress when nature calls?

Definitely use the bathroom before getting into your dress. Of course, that doesn't mean that the need will not strike later. If you're wearing a ball gown, ask a close friend to accompany you to the stall (best to try for a handicapped one, as they are more roomy). She should lift the dress up from the bottom rather than grabbing it and crunching the fabric, which will only create wrinkles. If you haven't bustled your train yet, just remember to keep it off the floor so you're not sweeping the floor on the way.

20. What is the etiquette of cake-cutting?

If your wedding is in any kind of catering facility such as a hotel, banquet hall, or restaurant, the staff will divvy up the cake so you won't have to worry about it. In a less formal setting such as at home or outdoors in a public park, you may need a few pointers. When cutting the cake, the groom's right hand goes over yours and you cut together. Cut a small taste from the bottom tier for the cake ceremony, and remove the top tier to save it for your anniversary (one month or one year). Cut the remaining portion into wedges starting with the highest layer, cutting slices from the outside rim into rectangular pieces. Slices should be as uniform as possible, about one to two inches thick and two to three inches deep.

21. How and when do I pay my wedding vendors?

Review each contract, call each vendor about two weeks prior to the wedding to confirm the balance payment amount, write out the checks, and place them in separate envelopes. Deliver pre-wedding payments yourself on the due dates. Hand the rest to the best man (or maid or matron of honor or whomever you've appointed) to distribute on the day of the wedding. If you plan on paying with plastic, call the credit card company ahead of time to get preapproved for the amount. Make sure to ask that copies of receipts be mailed to you.

22. What jewelry do you suggest for different types of necklines?

If your dress has an ornate bodice, then stick to earrings only, as too many details can be a distraction and take the focus away from your face and you as the bride. On a simple dress, however, try to have your necklace, if you're wearing one, flow with the neckline of your dress. On a V-neckline, go for a pendant to echo the line's V shape; on a scoop neckline, choose a rounded necklace that rests just below the throat; on a strapless gown, you can either wear a choker snug around the neck or layered strands of freshwater pearls interspersed with jewels and crystals.

23. Is it less expensive to have a destination wedding?

It all depends on how high-end you want to go. There is no definitive answer. Your guest list, the location, the venue and the time of the year/season are all factors to be taken into consideration. Considering that the average number of guests for at-home weddings is 150, chances are that only about half that number will be able to attend your destination wedding. Having a wedding at home can make you feel obliged to invite everybody you and your family knows, while more distant acquaintances are least likely to be able to make a destination wedding, so this helps keep the guest list smaller. Do extensive research on the wedding packages offered at different all-inclusive resorts to see what's included, check out airfare and room rates, and note which time of the year is the least expensive. An outdoor wedding means extra charges for tents, transportation, and outdoor toilet rentals, as well as air-conditioning or fans in tents to keep your guests cool and your flowers from wilting. Site and permit costs should be taken into account as well. Going away for a wedding can combine a family reunion and give both the bride's and groom's families a chance to spend time together and bond. It can also save on the honeymoon, as you can have an extended stay to enjoy time together after the guests have departed. For more details, see Chapter 3: Your Wedding, Your Way: *Your Venue, Your Destination, Your Style.*

24. My fiancé and I are a little confused about who should be hosting the rehearsal dinner.

Traditionally, the groom's family hosts the dinner, but these days there are no rules. Some couples prefer to host this dinner themselves or have both sets of parents co-host. The rehearsal dinner is often a very meaningful event and a good time to have your nearest and dearest gathered to celebrate more intimately with you. It usually takes place two nights or the night before the wedding and is an ideal time for the bride and groom to present gifts to party members and parents thanking them for their help.

25. I would like to have an authentic "traditional" wedding; could you please elaborate on what the criteria is for a "traditional bride?"

To have a truly traditional wedding with all the bells and whistles, here are some guidelines:

1. Your wedding gown needs to be classic, elegant, and timeless—nothing too trendy and none of that see-through and flashy stuff that is here today and gone tomorrow. Classic elements like silk, satin, and lace

have timeless charm, as do illusion necklines, bateau and Queen Anne necklines, and long or butterfly sleeves. A chapel or a cathedral train is essential to nail the traditional bridal look. Ideally, you would wear white or ivory. Shoes and other accessories must be simple and elegant.
2. Your invitations would be classic—the font elegant with solid strokes and straight lines—with custom details like a monogram, motifs, calligraphy, and lace details in metallic colors like gold, silver, or copper.
3. Your music should be soft and serene, with a healthy mix of timeless classics.
4. "Something old, something new, something borrowed, something blue" would be part of your wedding rituals.
5. A classic veil (preferably long) is a symbol of chastity; a circlet of wildflowers in your hair is reminiscent of old-world rituals. You could add either of these elements.
6. Accessories like pearls and gemstones in jewelry and tiaras, headpieces, hairpins, or headbands add classic touches to your overall look.
7. Traditional beauty is simple and feminine, never overdone. Simple makeup and a soft hairstyle, worn up or down, are the hallmarks of a traditional bride.
8. Follow the ritual of not being seen by the groom in your dress before the wedding, nor let him see your dress at all until you walk down the aisle.

You could even go further and add a silver coin in your shoe—a tradition every bride in the Victorian Age followed—believed to bring good luck and material success to the new couple after their wedding!

26. Can you please explain the meaning of "Something old, something new, something borrowed, something blue"?

This tradition comes from an old English rhyme, "Something old, something new, something borrowed, something blue, and a silver sixpence in her shoe," which refers to four objects that the bride adds to her wedding outfit or carries with her on the big day as good luck charms, plus the coin that is not remembered as often as part of the classic verse. Each has a particular meaning:

- *Something old* symbolizes your old life as a single woman.
- *Something new* illustrates your journey into a new life as a married woman.
- *Something borrowed* echoes the influences of your friends and family.
- *Something blue* is derived from the ancient Jewish traditions. This soothing color is believed to be a symbol of fidelity.
- *A silver sixpence in her shoe* is a wish for good fortune and prosperity.

27. Do you have any advice on the type of lingerie I should wear on my wedding night?

Your wedding day will be a long one, and since you will probably be worn out by the end of the day, you will be happier with lingerie that is simple to slip on. Go with a style that fits your personality, one that is a true reflection of you and that makes you feel confident and beautiful at the same time. Be okay with splurging a bit on your wedding lingerie and make sure it makes you feel gorgeous and sexy on this special night.

28. I would love to wear my mother's wedding dress, but it's somewhat plain and my style is more flamboyant. What do you recommend I do?

It is commendable that you would want to wear your mother's wedding dress. Here are some options that can help you personalize the dress to suit your personality:

- Have a seamstress add embellished details such as shimmery lace, crystals, or rhinestone work around the neckline, hemline, and even at the edges of the sleeves to add luxury without drowning it.
- Wear bold jewelry with your dress, such as a big bold necklace, chandelier earrings, or even a tiara. Accessories can add sparkle and compensate for an understated wedding gown.
- If it's a winter wedding, you could wear a fur cape, embroidered bolero jacket, or a beaded stole to add more style.
- Wear shoes with lace or beading or even a different color to add interest to your overall look.
- Choose an interesting hairstyle to add an extra dose of glamour and perhaps even dress it up with a complex floral or crystal headpiece.

29. We have a huge circle of close friends and relatives. How do I tell some of them that they're not in the wedding party?

The best way is to take care of this matter as soon as you announce your wedding, especially before they assume they will be in the wedding party. Tell them that as much as you would love to have them in the wedding party, you would rather they enjoy the wedding as guests instead. If your reason is that you would like to keep the wedding party small, then say exactly that. At all times, make sure you impart the fact that you value your relationship and would not want this to harm it in any way, and that you would love them involved in the wedding in any other way possible.

30. We're working on a really tight budget for our wedding. How do I tell my guests I would rather have cash than gifts (to help with my wedding expenses)?

Set up a wedding website where you will be sharing your wedding information and add "Gift cash toward ___" as one of the top options in the registry and link it to a designated bank account. Or, you could link your wedding registry to sites like Tendr.com, which make it easy for guests to give you cash gifts. And if by chance a guest were to ask you directly about your preferences, don't hesitate to let them know that you prefer contributions toward wedding expenses.

31. Our parents are sharing some of the expenses for our wedding. How do we tell them we would like something different than what they plan on giving us without hurting their feelings?

I suggest you handle the situation tactfully rather than locking horns with your families. To keep them happy, perhaps you could accommodate at least *some* of their ideas? Then let them know your wishes and what would make you both happy. It could be that you want a modern, relaxed wedding while your parents wish for you to have a traditional wedding. Whatever it is, let them know the things that you are unwilling to compromise on, but before doing so, let them know which of their suggestions you would love to include in your wedding. After that, share with them your plans and present your final idea. Request that they understand and convey your gratitude on all they are helping with to make sure your wedding day is memorable and beautiful.

32. I have a cousin who has offered to bake my wedding cake, but I have my heart set on a cake vendor who will be better able to translate my idea and give me what I would like. How do I get out of this without hurting my cousin's feelings?

We all have someone we know who thinks they are the best baker, the most savvy photographer, or the best wedding planner. No doubt they may be great at what they do, but you may have your own reasons for not wanting to give them that responsibility. Involving a relative or a friend can be sticky. It means you have to watch everything and be cautious about what you say for fear of upsetting them. Some can also be opinionated and unwilling to see your point. Either way, you are better off saying "no" from the get-go to their offer. Be diplomatic and let them know that as much as you would love to have them handle the task, you have already committed to another vendor. Tell them you would rather they enjoy the wedding as your guest instead of working all day. This way you are clearly conveying how much you value their presence and appreciate them.

33. How do we keep our wedding guest list small enough to fit our budget and say no to guests our parents want to invite?

The best thing is to give your parents a specific number of guests they can invite so they may, at their own discretion, prioritize who gets to be on their list. Stick to this number even though it is tough for you to say no to your dear ones. After all, you want to be honest about what you can afford and you know that stretching your budget is not an option. Besides, your wedding is really about celebrating with people who matter most to you.

Here are some questions you can ask as you're preparing your own guest list:

- Have either of you met this person? If not, go ahead and eliminate them.
- Have either of you talked with this person in the past year? No? Then this person will not feel offended if not invited.
- Were you invited to their wedding? No? It's perfectly fine to reciprocate.
- If this is an office co-worker, do you spend time outside of work with them? If not, then they are just an acquaintance, and need not make the list.

34. I would love to have bridesmaids. However, I know what a burden that can be for my friends. My own budget is exhausted and I'm not sure I can help pay for their dresses. Any advice?

The financial burden put on bridesmaids is considerable. This is one of the reasons many dread being asked to be one. They not only have to pay for a dress, but also accessories, the bridal shower, bachelorette party, and gifts for the bride among other things. If your own budget doesn't allow any contribution toward their expenses, then perhaps you may want to keep your dress selection reasonable or even think outside the box by giving them the option to mix and match pieces instead of having them all commit to wearing similar outfits. Provide them with a shortlist of choices along with the color you would like so they can have the freedom to choose a dress they can wear again.

35. Do I have to pay for my bridesmaids' dresses?

Traditionally, the attendants pay for their own outfits, but do be considerate and choose dresses that fit their budgets. You can certainly help by paying for their accessories or hair and makeup. And if you absolutely must see your bridesmaids in a designer label, then be prepared to pitch in.

36. What questions should I be asking my caterer so there are no surprises?

Your wedding menu and the talent and reliability of your caterer are just as important as your wedding décor and the rest of your wedding planning. Before you decide on your caterer, do the following:

- Ask if they have worked in a similar venue before. Ask about their experience handling weddings and whether they are able to handle weddings of a similar nature and scale as yours.

- Go with caterers that come with good references and recommendations. How have other brides' experiences been with this caterer?

- Find out their service charges and what they include. Catering is not only about providing the food, but may also include setting up, serving, cake slicing, and cleaning up after service. Will there be extra charges for cutlery, glassware, and tableware? Make sure the costs fit your budget.

- Ask how many staff will be involved at the wedding and what roles they will play. Will they be refilling glasses at the tables, or will guests be collecting their beverages at a designated station? For a formal sit-down meal, the ideal server-to-guest ratio is one or two waiters per twelve guests, and for a buffet-style meal, it is one per twenty-five guests.

- Ask which foods will be ready-to-serve and which will be prepared on site. Certain foods require assembling or finishing just prior to being served. Foods such as crisp and fried foods need to be prepared right before service or they will be soggy and unappetizing.

- Ask for a tasting session with your caterer and make sure the dishes you approve at the tasting session will be the exact ones that will be served at your wedding.

- Ask how many other weddings they will be handling on the same day as yours. Vendors who take on more orders than they can handle often fall short of your expectations. Besides, if they are only working on your wedding, then you can expect a more personal service.

37. Can I have a cash bar, or is that inappropriate?

Think about it: Would you invite someone to your home and charge for drinks? You got it: The answer is no. If budget is an issue, then consider limiting your alcohol to beer and wine. Another alternative is purchasing your own alcohol, which allows you to shop around for the best prices. However, do check with your caterer or the facility beforehand, as they may charge a corkage fee.

38. Do we have to mention our parents on the invitations if we are paying for the entire wedding?

No, but if the two of you feel close to your respective parents, by all means list them out of respect and to avoid hurt feelings. Keep in mind that the names that appear on the invitation indicate those hosting the event, not necessarily the people who are paying for the event.

39. How do I decide who will be my maid or matron of honor?

Save this key supportive role for the relative or friend who means the most to you. Should there be a tie, think of the responsibilities, such as arranging a date to have all bridesmaids' gowns fitted, hosting the shower, greeting the officiant, helping out during the dinner reception, etc. Who among these will come through for you when the situation calls for a calm demeanor and positive outcome? That is the person you want to be your maid or matron of honor.

40. How do we ask our family for financial help with our wedding?

Each of you should set up a meeting with your own parents—it's only natural for in-laws-to-be to feel squeamish discussing money in front of future family members. When asking, try to keep your tone cheerful yet neutral. Describe the type of wedding you envision, your projected budget, and what you and your fiancé can afford. Then ask them if they're planning to lend a hand. If the amount they offer is less than you expected, and they don't bother explaining, be understanding and don't insist on an explanation. They may have financial setbacks you do not know about.

41. I ordered my dress, and when it arrived six months later, I was really disappointed. I'd like to cancel my order. What options do I have?

This is actually quite a normal occurrence. It's been a long time since you chose your dress, and months later it may not look as ideal as you remembered. In the months since your order, your dress has achieved a status of perfection in your head. Many brides panic at their first fitting. They go home, think about it, and it gets worse. But when they see the dress again, it's usually fine. If it isn't and after a few days you still don't like the dress, ask your consultant if some things can be altered such as the neckline or sleeves or if embellishments can be added. However, if you want big changes such as a different bodice or a different color, you may have to start shopping all over again and forfeit your deposit or full payment. Wedding dresses are generally specially ordered for you, and most stores and establishments have a no-return policy, which is to be expected. Alterations can make a dress fit well, so talk to your bridal consultant to go over your options.

42. I'm very conscious of my arms, but sleeves are not in fashion. What do you suggest I do?

First of all, that is not true. We're seeing more and more sleeves in wedding gowns today. Short or long sheer lace sleeves especially have always been in fashion. If you aren't fond of showing off your arms, then certainly choose a gown with sleeves. Some types of sleeves may be difficult to wear because the combination of a fitted bodice and sleeves means the dress will be very restricted. Not only that, but certain types of sleeves do not allow much movement when dancing, especially if a bride is shorter than her groom. However, not all sleeves are made equal, and not all sleeves are slimming, either. To achieve a slimmer look, opt for butterfly sleeves or short cap sleeves, which are definitely relevant and timeless, and help shift focus from your shoulders and upper arms.

43. How can I pick colors for my wedding?

Your venue can be one of the most, if not the most, important factor that will determine the colors for your wedding. Below are some tips for narrowing down your choices:

- Look at the colors already incorporated in the space where you will be married. If there are more gold and warm tones, then go with warm colors. If there are more white and silver tones, then go with cool colors.

- Pick your main signature color that will be the central theme of your wedding, and then match other hues around this so they complement each other.

- Study color combos used at other weddings, artwork displays in galleries, or hues in paintings you admire. What are you drawn toward?

- Use the color wheel as your resource when pairing colors. Note that colors opposite of each other on the wheel complement each other. Feel free to match neutrals with either warm or cold tones, and use metallic colors as accents.

- When picking colors, take into consideration flowers that will be in season, since they are so much more affordable.

For more, see Chapter 11: Color in Your Wedding.

44. I would like to write my own vows. As a writer yourself, could you guide me, please?

Your vows are personal. They are an expression of your love for the person you are about to share your life with. Be truthful and pour your feelings into your vows. Ask yourself the following questions as you write:

- What do you want the tone of your vows to be? You can discuss this with your fiancé so that you can decide together. If one of you writes in a very serious tone, while the other person is humorous, the latter may be misconstrued as being disrespectful even though that was never the intention.
- Decide on the length. Vows are usually no more than two minutes long.
- Start with a basic statement by addressing your loved one, beginning with your fiancé's name followed by your feelings about his strengths, the qualities you most love about him, and his caring nature.
- Continue with personal and specific promises you would like to make, which can include statements about how you would show your love and commitment.
- End with a sentiment about the eternal bond, such as "as long as we both shall live."

When done, practice saying the vows aloud. Do you feel awkward? How will they sound to your fiancé and guests? Time your vows to make sure they're just the right length. Start writing your vows early so you have time to make changes and practice. Above all make sure they feel genuine and authentic, words expressed from deep within your heart.

45. How formal is formal? I'd like to introduce an old-world feel into my very traditional wedding. What are the guidelines when dressing my wedding party in this case?

Weddings have seen so many changes over the years. Today, there are no hard and fast rules. However, here are some general guidelines for what was traditionally expected from yesteryear:

Most Formal Daytime:

- *Bride*—Long white/ivory dress, train and veil. Gloves optional.
- *Bride's attendants*—Long dress, matching shoes. Gloves are bride's option.
- **Groom, his attendants, bride's father or stepfather**—Cutaway coat, striped trousers, pearl-gray waistcoat, white stiff shirt, turndown collar with gray-and-black striped four-in-hand tie or wing collar with ascot, gray gloves, black socks and shoes.
- **Mothers and stepmothers of the couple**—Long or short dress; hat, veil or hair ornament; gloves.
- *Groom's father*—He may wear the same costume as the groom and his attendant, especially if he is to stand in the receiving line.

Most Formal Evening:

- *Bride*—Long white/ivory dress, train and veil. Gloves optional.
- *Bride's attendants*—Long dress, matching shoes. Gloves are bride's option.
- **Groom, his attendants, bride's father or stepfather**—Black tailcoat and trousers, white pique waistcoat, starched bosom shirt, wing collar, white bow tie, white gloves, black silk socks, black patent leather shoes, or black smooth-toe kid shoes.

- *Mothers and stepmothers of the couple*—Long evening or dinner dress, with veil or hair ornament, or dressy short cocktail dress with small hat; gloves.
- *Groom's father*—He may wear the same costume as the groom and his attendant, especially if he is to stand in the receiving line.

Semiformal Evening:

- *Bride*—Long white/ivory dress, short veil. Gloves optional.
- *Bride's attendants*—Same length and degree of formality as bride's dress.
- **Groom, his attendants, bride's father or stepfather**—Winter: black tuxedo. Summer: white jacket. Pleated pique soft shirt, black cummerbund, black bow tie, black patent-leather or kid shoes.
- *Mothers and stepmothers of the couple*—Long or short dress; gloves; head covering optional.
- *Groom's father*—He may wear the same costume as the groom and his attendant, especially if he is to stand in the receiving line.

Informal Daytime:

- *Bride*—Short afternoon dress, cocktail dress, or suit.
- *Bride's attendants*—Same style as bride.
- **Groom, his attendants, bride's father or stepfather**—Winter: dark suit. Summer: white linen jacket with dark trousers, or navy or charcoal jacket with white trousers. Hot climate: white suit, soft shirt, conservative four-in-hand tie.
- *Mothers and stepmothers of the couple*—Short afternoon or cocktail dress.
- *Groom's father*—He may wear the same costume as the groom and his attendant, especially if he is to stand in the receiving line.

46. My gown was custom-ordered to my size. However, now that the gown has arrived, I am told I will have to pay for alterations. Is this normal?

Unless you have a written contract that says alterations are included in the price, you are liable for alteration charges. More than 90 percent of brides who buy a new wedding dress, custom-made or not, need alterations. Furthermore, between the time you placed your order and its arrival, your weight may have fluctuated slightly, hence you would need at least minor alterations to ensure a proper and flattering fit. Wedding dress alterations are complex and time-consuming and can involve hours of labor. Make sure to schedule your final fitting session closer to your wedding day in case any final adjustments are needed.

47. Any advice on what to do when planning my honeymoon?

If you're planning your honeymoon at a distant or overseas location, then do your homework far in advance. Perhaps get firsthand input from a friend or relative who has been there and can advise you on what they enjoyed most about the place and what to avoid. If possible, consult with an international expert who is familiar with the region. Your honeymoon planning should start as soon as the wedding date is set. Decide on a location both you and your fiancé have always envisioned as your ideal honeymoon experience, and explore your options. Start inquiring about dates and availability as soon as possible, keeping in mind weather conditions and other factors at the destination at the time.

If you're having a destination wedding and are already in a beautiful place after the event, then it could be the perfect launch for your honeymoon and a much more relaxing experience for you. You could easily go to nearby places and explore. For instance, if you're getting married in Florence, you could rent a private car or take the train to

Rome, Assisi, and Sienna, and spend your honeymoon exploring and enjoying other Italian cities. Or, a wedding in Aspen during the winter months could lead straight into a ski trip.

Definitely do your homework, research, and pack your luggage based on the weather and available resources. Some tropical places may require that you pack mosquito repellant and bug spray, while some places may have dress restrictions for visiting some of their tourist spots. Check with your hotel for what will be provided and expect that it may not always be possible to buy some things that you require. Create a checklist in advance, and above all, don't forget the essentials. If traveling overseas, carry photocopies of your passports and other documents on you at all times.

Whatever you do, make sure to actually make time for your honeymoon. Life can get busy once you are married and resume your normal routines, so this is your chance to truly enjoy your newly married life and celebrate each other. Your honeymoon will give you that perfect start to face your new life together. Make up your mind to relax and enjoy your time!

48. My mother-in-law-to-be has threatened to not attend the reception if her ex-husband's new wife will be there. How should I deal with this awkward family drama?

Family issues such as these are not uncommon. I suggest your fiancé has separate conversations with both sets of parents in advance and see if a comfortable solution can be found for all. Perhaps separate their seating and create space between them. Make strategic plans with your wedding planner, venue coordinator, and photographer letting them know about any tricky family dynamics so they can help minimize any potential awkward encounters, and come up with a way to give everyone a chance to enjoy and be part of the celebrations. If your mother-in-law makes this her hill to die on, that

is her choice. Your fiancé's father has the right to bring his wife, just as his ex-wife may bring her own partner, if she has one.

49. I've been to weddings where family members gave lengthy toasts and even some inappropriate ones. How to handle these situations?

It's typical for hosts and close family members to give a welcome toast. However, to make sure they're not long and inappropriate, plan ahead. Discuss your expectations regarding the subject matter of their toast. Politely let them know you are honored, but because you wish to give everyone a fair chance and to allow guests time to enjoy mingling with each other, you have decided to give each person a time limit—ideally, less than five minutes. Make sure the person toasting is close enough to the bandleader or DJ, who can grab the microphone in case things get out of hand.

50. My heart is set on a beautiful dress I found online on a designer's website but the dress is not available in my size. Is there any way to let it out while still keeping the style intact?

Absolutely! This is actually a simpler solution than many think. I suggest finding a good seamstress, ideally one who is familiar with wedding gown and evening gown alterations, and discuss options with her. Many wedding dresses have generous seam allowances at the sides as well as the center back that can be let out about two to three sizes. Beyond that, your seamstress can open up the back of the dress and create corset ties, which is actually a very beautiful option.

In case the back must be opened very low into the hip area, then she can create a modesty piece. The modesty piece is a piece of fabric matching the dress, or one with matching embellishments, that is sewn into the dress or is made detachable and placed behind the corset lacing in the back. This is especially needed if the corset opening goes down very low, as it gives coverage so that the bride's undergarments do not show.

Altering your gown to have a corset back and/or a modesty piece easily allows you more than enough room to open up your purchased gown by several sizes.

51. What are the appropriate outfits to wear to a wedding when you're a guest?

Depending on what your invitation says and the type of wedding, here are some general dress codes:

WHITE TIE:

- *Men*—Tuxedo and a white bow tie.
- *Women*—Floor-length ball gown.

BLACK TIE:

- *Men*—Tuxedo with a black bow tie.
- *Women*—Formal dress or chic evening gown.

DRESSY CASUAL:

- *Men*—Any outfit that is formal and dressy .
- *Women*—A nice skirt and a silk blouse or a pretty cocktail dress.

COCKTAIL ATTIRE:

- *Men*—Fanciest tailored suit.
- *Women*—An elegant dress and heels.

Formal/ Black Tie Optional:

- *Men*—Black suit and tie, or a tuxedo.
- *Women*—A formal dress or a really chic jumpsuit.

Casual: Although this means "anything goes," it doesn't mean you can show up in shorts and flip-flops.

- *Men*—Pants with a button-down shirt.
- *Women*—A casual dress or a nice skirt and a blouse.

Beach Formal:

- *Men*—Light khakis or pants and a casual shirt.
- *Women*—Nice summer dress or a pretty cocktail dress.

52. Could you please share styling mistakes I should avoid?

Here are a few things about style that a bride should be mindful of on her big day:

1. Don't get too carried away and overdo your hair and makeup. Look like yourself.
2. Make sure the hem of your dress is not too long to avoid tripping.
3. If wearing curls in your hair, make sure they are not lacquered in hair spray and appear stiff.
4. If getting a tan, make sure your skin does not burn or seem too orange from a spray tan gone awry.
5. Decide what story you want to tell in the theme, in the décor, in your fashion. Create an atmosphere that reflects your style.

6. Don't be afraid to wear color—at your rehearsal dinner *and* on your wedding day.

7. Don't worry about losing too much weight. Your nerves will naturally speed up your metabolism as your wedding day approaches.

8. Don't look stiff in your photographs.

9. Do something to calm your nerves on the day of your wedding, such as working out in the morning, hanging out on the beach, or doing yoga with your bridesmaids.

10. Be classic. Be unique. Be you. There is no need to follow trends others expect of you.

53. How do I keep little children and young ones happy on the day?

At a wedding where there are children of various ages, here are some fun suggestions to keep them occupied, interested, and happy:

- Set up an arts-and-crafts room. Bring a roll of butcher paper, crayons, markers, glitter, and glue, and ask them to make a special card for the bride and groom. Or, set up projects like painting birdcages or making jewelry. Be sure to supply smocks to protect their party clothes.

- Encourage future journalists. Give each child a goody bag filled with age-appropriate toys, candy, a pretend or disposable camera, and a notebook so they can pretend they are reporters covering a big event.

- Pack a lunch. The secret to keeping children entertained is to feed them so parents can enjoy their dinners. Give each child a lunch-box filled with peanut butter-and-jelly finger sandwiches, crackers, grapes, and carrot sticks, along with a finger puppet or a small toy. Hire a baby-sitter to take the children outdoors or to play in a room where they can watch movies.

- Create kid-specific centerpieces when seating children at their own table. These can include colorful lollipops in terracotta pots filled with pebbles to hold the treats in place.

- Assemble a chorus. Send a CD recording of a song to all of the children attending the wedding along with a note asking them to learn the tune and prepare to sing it during the ceremony.

Note: The above are based on my personal experiences. They are my opinions only. You and your loved ones may have other thoughts. Go with what you feel is best for you . . .

CHAPTER TWENTY-SIX

101 WEDDING TIPS

1. Use embellishments to draw the eye to your beautiful face. Elegant embellishments on the bodice draw the eye upward, adding a glow to your skin, eyes, and hair.

2. Corset styling not only offers plenty of support, it also holds everything in place. Corsets are great for plus-size brides.

3. Basque waists give a nice lengthening effect to the front of the dress.

4. Whether full and constructed, or soft and deconstructed, the A-line dress is the all-time biggest problem-solver.

5. A long veil can add height and allure, and so can a tiara.

6. Wearing your hair up makes you look taller.

7. Lace sleeves can elongate your arms and make them look very elegant. Long satin sleeves accentuate the arms and make them look thicker.

8. Keeping arms bare actually minimizes their size.

9. Stiff fabrics tend to smother large chests and make them look bulky.

10. Make a grand entrance but an even grander exit! The back of your gown must be distinctive and original because that is the part of the dress typically in the spotlight while you are exchanging your vows.

11. The best way to put on a ball gown is to position the petticoat under the center of your dress, then step into both at the same time.

12. Put on your accessories only after you're fully dressed.

13. Never underestimate the importance of lingerie. Beautiful underwear is part of a woman's personality so don't save it for a special day. You want to feel beautiful every day to keep your man interested in you.

14. The bigger the headpiece, the smaller the earrings.

15. The hem of your dress should be a half-inch shorter in front rather than the same length all the way around to avoid your shoes getting caught in the hem.

16. When choosing your photographer, look at their ability to tell a "story". View the complete album of one wedding, from start to finish, rather than random samples from many weddings the photographer has shot.

17. When picking your reception venue, take into account the size of the parking lot and number of restrooms as well as the capacity of the ballroom. The rule of thumb is one parking space for every two guests and one toilet for every twenty guests.

18. Keep the bouquet you carried down the aisle to press and preserve, and ask your florist to provide a "toss bouquet" designed especially for this ritual.

19. Insure your wedding day against anything and everything that may go wrong, from your dress mishaps to bad weather to stolen presents. Make sure to go through a reputable insurance agency.

20. Presents have a way of disappearing, so set up a gift table near the door of your reception room and have an attendant man it at all times.

21. Provide a map to your out-of-town guests with clear details that include distance and driving time to the venue and hotel information.

22. Use unexpected colors for bridesmaids rather than the classic champagnes and pastels. Navy blue, ruby, even burgundy look smart, expensive, and sleek on everyone.

23. A long coat over your gown is a great way to cover for a more formal ceremony and a stylish way to travel outside during the cooler weather.

24. For open-toe shoes, choose a polish that blends with the bottom of your gown, such as iridescent white. A dramatic color draws your attention down and makes you look shorter.

25. Decide on your hairstyle before choosing your headpiece and veil. The veil comes off after the ceremony, so your hair is what everyone sees.

26. Keep a second pair of shoes handy in case your feet swell, preferably shoes with a lower heel and a half-size larger.

27. If wearing glasses on your wedding day, make sure they have non-reflective lenses to avoid flash glare in your wedding pictures.

28. Fragrances should be worn in layers, starting with your bath gel, then body lotion, and finally apply the actual fragrance to pulse points—between your breasts, on your throat behind your ears, on your wrists, in the crooks of your elbows, at the backs of your knees, and on your ankles.

29. Keep an emergency beauty kit handy for touch-ups at regular intervals during your wedding day. Include a comb, hair spray, pressed powder, mascara, and lipstick.

30. Anchor your headpiece with bobby pins or a discreet pin curl that's been treated with firm hair spray for extra hold to make sure it stays in place.

31. Shop for your shoes at the end of the day, when your foot is at its largest. Wear your shoes around the house to break them in. There's nothing worse than feet that hurt!

32. A good-fitting shoe must meet the following criteria: Your heel should fit snugly in back, and the ball of your foot should rest on the widest part of the shoe. Make sure you can wiggle your toes and that they don't push or bulge against the front of your shoe.

33. Shop for your wedding dress on weekdays to avoid the crowds. This way you are assured more time and attention with your salesperson. Or, if shopping during the weekend, make sure your appointment is the first one of the day so you won't experience any delay due to a salesperson's backed-up schedule.

34. If you would like your fitter to help you get dressed and bustle your train on the wedding day, ask about her availability in advance. Many will gladly provide this extra service for a fee.

35. Once you bring the dress home, suspend it on a rod and leave it in its garment bag, leaving the bag slightly open to prevent mustiness.

36. Have your maid or matron of honor watch and learn how your hairstylist puts your veil in, so she knows how to remove your veil without destroying your hairstyle.

37. Keep white chalk handy for on-the-spot touch-ups to your gown. Simply rub it on to cover up small stains.

38. Link your stationery with a common thread. From invites to menus, all should flow well including color, font, or paper stock. You want to create a consistent memory to tie it all together.

39. If your invitations include response cards, remember to include stamps for the response card envelope.

40. The longer the train of your wedding gown, the looser your bouquet. This doesn't necessarily mean a cascade, but just less uptight flowers.

41. Let your florist know that you will not accept wilted flowers or unopened buds. Insist on blooming flowers for the big day.

42. Hand-tied stems are less costly than carefully constructed bouquets, and sculpted centerpieces are more costly than loose-cut flowers arranged in vases.

43. Try black-and-white film for iconic moments. The timeless quality lends itself to scenes such as your walk down the aisle, and candid shots behind the scenes when you are not made-up and as you're getting ready.

44. When wearing a sleeveless, dress do not press your arms to your sides, as this makes your upper arms appear larger than they are in pictures.

45. It's not enough to know what you want your DJ to play. Let them know what NOT to play. Be specific and provide them with a play/don't play list.

46. Make sure you have enough bathrooms for your guests and consider hiring an attendant to make sure the stalls are presentable at all times.

47. Assign a friend or relative as the go-to contact person for when guests have any questions or concerns. Provide them with this person's mobile phone number.

48. Make sure to serve hors d'oeuvres that can be eaten in one bite to avoid potential aggravation and embarrassment as guests try to eat oversized hors d'oeuvres while standing.

49. Hire a wedding planner for the day. You will enjoy your wedding day so much more knowing that there is a dedicated person overseeing all the activities and guests.

50. Invest in extra service so your guests feel pampered and advise waiters to fold napkins and pull out chairs for the ladies.

51. Don't wait too long to cut the cake. Guests can get cranky waiting for this final ritual, especially if they have a long drive home.

52. Make sure the runner on the aisle is flat, especially if it's laid over carpeting. If the runner is laid on wood, make sure it's fastened properly to avoid any mishaps when making your big walk down the aisle.

53. Consider your guests' food requirements and restrictions when planning your menu. Have alternative menus to accommodate those with food allergies or dietary restrictions for health, religious, or personal reasons.

54. Choose music that is irresistible and songs that everyone loves. This will help create a wonderful energy and invite guests to dance.

55. Don't forget the bar. Guests love hanging out at a bar, so be creative with your drinks and create a fun, laid-back atmosphere for guests to enjoy.

56. Check to make sure all the technology works. Your Apple product may not sync with your speakers, and the plugs may not fit in the sockets. Don't assume everything will work at the venue—test it all out before the event begins.

57. Make sure your venue has a full-length mirror in your bridal suite.

58. Bring a steamer with you on your wedding day for any last-minute touch-ups that may be necessary.

59. Make sure to check your list of must-haves a couple of days before the wedding: a copy of your vows, your marriage license, programs, flower-girl basket, ring-bearer pillow, favors, table numbers, etc.

60. For a winter wedding, consider chic options such as capes or fur stoles to add glamour, shawls for a sexy look, or floor-length coats and removable bolero jackets.

61. If you're suffering from honeymoon destination indecision, the best thing to do is for each to prepare a wish list: tropical climate, ski resort, water sports, road trip across Europe—whatever you desire. Then compare and combine your lists into one to make a decision that will make both of you happy.

62. Considering a honeymoon destination during the off-season affords you better prices for flights and hotels.

63. When booking your room, make sure you know the travel industry lingo. Did you know that an oceanfront and an ocean-view room are two different things? The first refers to a room smack on the beach, the second a room that affords you a view of the ocean from afar (you may even have to crane your neck!) that is possibly not even a full view of the ocean.

64. At an upscale hotel, consider booking a room on the club floor as it has its own concierge, a lounge, and access to late afternoon cocktails and hors d'oeuvres and breakfast. This would possibly save you money in the long run.

65. If traveling overseas for your honeymoon, it's best to exchange money at a bank or hotel of your destination rather than at home since the rate of exchange is more favorable in the country whose currency you need.

66. Make sure to inform your credit card provider if you're going on an overseas trip to avoid any sticky problems and make sure they do not place a hold on your cards.

YOUR BRIDAL STYLE

67. Avoid paying your vendors or for your services with cash or check. Pay with a credit card instead so that you have a valid record of each payment and have the added protection of credit card companies within an allotted time frame, normally sixty days. Paying with cash affords you no recourse in case things go wrong.

68. Always check references and only deal with companies you know to be reputable.

69. Getting detailed contracts and agreements is the best way to safeguard against any hidden fees or unkept promises. Be sure to read all the fine print, including cancellation terms and refund policies. Keep your copies in a safe place.

70. Booking your reception venue for Saturday night is most costly. To save money, consider Friday or Sunday night, Saturday or Sunday afternoon, or a weekday or weeknight.

71. Morning or afternoon weddings call for lighter, less expensive fare, and allow you to save on the food as well.

72. To avoid paying an additional location fee, consider having your officiant perform the ceremony at your reception site.

73. Save on restaurant costs by hosting a luncheon or rehearsal dinner in your or one of your parents' homes.

74. To take pressure off and look your best on your wedding day, consider hiring a professional hairstylist and makeup artist to come to your home.

75. Never pretend to be someone you're not. Approach your wedding and all related activities as an extension of your true personality. Be true to who you are, and even though it's perfectly okay to glam yourself up, never try to change your identity completely.

76. If writing your own vows, be honest, be brief, and use simple phrases without being overly sentimental. Write your vows ahead of time and feel free to let your partner know what you plan to say. Practice saying them in a way that sounds more conversational and less contrived.

77. Decide on your budget and your guest list before you begin planning your wedding. All other details will be determined by these two factors.

78. When inviting friends or relatives to be in your wedding party, select only those you know for sure you can count on, as you will be relying heavily on them for help and support. Fear of hurting someone's feelings is not a good reason when making your choice.

79. To cut the cake, place your hand on the cake knife with the groom's hand over yours. The first slice is placed on a plate and your groom feeds you a small piece then receives a bite from you, his bride. The remainder of the cake is cut by waiters and distributed to guests.

80. Your thank-you notes need not be lengthy, but should include a mention of the gift by name and how you will use it in your new home. If it was a monetary gift, mention what you plan to do with it without having to state the amount.

81. Make sure your ceremony satisfies both your feelings, your beliefs, and your family traditions, as it is the heart of your wedding and sets the tone for the entire day. The order of your processional and recessional will depend on the type of ceremony you're having—religious, civil, or military—so make sure to go over details with your officiant. Interfaith couples may choose to have a clergy member from each faith present.

82. Make sure to select in-season, locally grown flowers, since they are more plentiful and less expensive. Most flowers are fuller, hardier, available in more variety, and less expensive during their peak growing time.

83. The flowers you wear or carry must complement your personality and the gown you are wearing.

84. The shape and style of the bridesmaids' flowers should complement the bridal bouquet and flatter each attendant's stature.

85. Put extra pins in your veil and secure it so it does not fall off. Some veils weigh more than they appear to, particularly when they are long. Someone may step on your veil and cause your head to be pulled back, so do pin the veil on tightly.

86. When posing for pictures, angle your shoulders toward the camera, then turn your head to look straight at it. This helps smooth out neck wrinkles and makes you look trimmer.

87. Check your teeth closely just before the ceremony for any small particles of food or lipstick on your teeth, as it will look bad when captured on film.

88. Avoid getting too tan for your wedding. There is nothing worse than not looking like your normal self in your photographs, or tan lines showing up under a sheer wedding dress.

89. Have a friend or family member at your wedding with sewing skills. You never know when you will need their assistance.

90. If traveling with your wedding dress, check with your airline to see if they would be willing to store it in the first-class cabin wardrobe. If not, then pack your dress in a hard-sided maximum-size carry-on cabin suitcase.

91. If you're having your dress custom-made, ask your bridal consultant about having a bra and corset built in.

92. Hide an heirloom in your gown, such as a family locket sewn into the hem or an antique handkerchief stitched into the waist seam.

93. Personalize your cocktails. If you love martinis, create a martini menu and name the drinks after important events, people, or things in your lives.

94. Honor family members no longer with you. For our bride Elizabeth, we created a heart-shaped piece out of monogrammed cuffs from her father's shirt and stitched it into her bodice.

95. Save your train. Instead of preserving your entire dress, snip off the train and turn it into a pillow for your first child's nursery.

96. Find a fragrance to match your flowers. Look for a perfume or have a perfume custom-blended based on the scents in your bouquet.

97. Ask that your shower have a theme. If you or your fiancé love to read, have a book shower. If you're both fans of fine wine, suggest a wine shower.

98. Make sure to eat something on the day of your wedding, since you will need energy to stand on your feet for any length of time.

99. Enlist the help of a friend or bridesmaid to act as a buffer throughout the planning process as well as during the big day when you might need help smoothing out some awkward situations.

100. Make sure your florist sees a photo of your gown so your bouquet doesn't cover or overpower your dress.

101. Spread words of love. One way to create a romantic table is to adorn the runners with poetry. A bride I worked with had different love poems handwritten along the edges of the runners at her tables.

Final Thoughts

THE EVOLUTION OF BRIDAL FASHION AND FINAL THOUGHTS . . .

The wedding gown has evolved drastically over centuries of cultural and stylistic evolution.

When I launched my St. Pucchi collection in 1985, the look was extremely conservative and traditional. Bodices were somewhat short and attached to the skirt at the natural waist. High-waisted gowns, also known as the empire style, were also in vogue and worn by the fashionable brides in those days. Necklines were higher to give more coverage in keeping with the traditional standards of the day.

This followed the Victorian standards of morality, which stated that the ideal woman should be modest, charming, feminine, acquiescent, and respectable . . . and completely dependent on the male! In that era, fashion dictated that a woman's dress therefore must clearly reflect her subscription to these values, and her dress must camouflage her physical form, covering as much skin as possible. Along with that, she wore the most massive, cumbersome hoops, which also had the most absurd widths, reaching out several feet on each side. A lavish dress would layer at least three or four full skirts with flounces and ruches and incorporate at least 1,100 yards of fabric for a single gown! The ideal big wedding took on theatrical proportions, and to undress one of these brides was a complicated enterprise that had to be planned in advance, like moving a house!

With the advent of railroad travel, a more practical way of dressing was required, and narrower skirts and rear bustles became the rage. Even with the lighter loads the women carried, the simplest dress still weighed about twenty, pounds if not more. Propriety still required that the bride wear a tightly corseted bodice and be hidden under a frilly outer bodice with a high neck and long sleeves. A narrow waist, tight bodice, and graceful, full skirt with a train was the accepted classic bridal silhouette.

In the 1920s, when the Nineteenth Amendment was passed in the United States, finally granting women personhood and the right to vote, women awoke to their newfound freedom. The bridal look changed and became less fussy and more functional. The stock market crash in 1929 gave rise to Depression brides, who had to make do with their best dresses to be married in. Brides took cues from Hollywood glamour as the film industry flourished and provided an antidote to the painful times enveloped in fantasy.

The 1930s saw new bridal fashions take precedence. When Princess Marina of Greece wed the Duke of Kent in 1934, she wore a slim sheath of white and silver lamé with fitted sleeves and a Watteau court train that cascaded from her shoulders to pool on the floor. It was beautiful and elegant and captured the hearts of every woman when the image spread all over the world via the newly published magazine, *So You're Going to Be Married*, which launched in 1934.

This magazine was renamed *The Bride's Magazine* in 1936 and would eventually be called *Bride's*, which exists to this day. Fashionable women began to wear simpler gowns resembling narrow, ionic columns, hence the term "column dress." In a dramatic departure from the wide skirts of the past, which concealed the true shape of a woman's body—especially in the days when women wore panniers that extended the width of the skirts at the sides, even up to a few feet at times—the slim silhouette came as a shock to the bridal industry and brides turned with anticipation to Bride's magazine as their bible for guidance and advice on the latest bridal fashions as well as on every aspect of their wedding.

Fashion changed drastically with World War II, which lasted from 1939 to 1945, and had a profound effect on the way women dressed. Necessity demanded that restrictions be placed on luxury industries, including bridal manufacturing. "Frivolous" dressing was banned, hosiery was out of production, and bridal fabrics became scarce, resulting in brides having to forsake a traditional wedding and cut out all the trimmings. Bridal gowns were either rented or passed down among friends and relatives. Challenges of all kinds affected the bridal arena.

The post-war era of the 1950s once again reflected a change in values through fashion. A modern reinterpretation of the nineteenth-century-style ball gown emerged. The look was either an ankle-length, train-less ball gown made of nylon lace, organdy, or point d'esprit over stiff crinoline and a short, full bouffant veil, or a full-skirted, full-length ball gown with a tight, form-fitted bodice showing off a tiny waist. The classic Cinderella-like fashion gave rise to emporiums devoted to the bridal industry, and custom-tailored all-white wedding gowns that would be worn only once became all the rage. Formal weddings became the standard.

The 1960s questioned the traditional values of a wedding. A whole generation of anti-war, anti-fashion, anti-conservative but pro-love and pro-peace brides uprooted the longstanding bridal traditions to embrace earthier ceremonies that celebrated their modern values. The bridal look gravitated toward cotton caftans and eyelet peasant smocks, and muslin and cotton lace replaced the tulle and silk ball gowns of their parents' generation. Young couples vowed, in their own words, to share their lives and had evening ceremonies on beaches instead of at chapels and cathedrals at noon.

However, despite this new direction, many brides could not help but be emotionally drawn to the past and honor their dream of a traditional wedding. Most of the wedding gowns worn in the 1960s and 1970s were white and floor-length, demure, covered up, and unwavering in their styling. There were two basic shapes: the narrow empire or princess line, and the full-skirted ball gown with fitted bodice. Necklines were strictly cut not to be lower than two and a half inches from the hollow at the base of the throat.

All that changed in the 1980s, and bridal gowns became more fashionable as innovative fabrics such as point d'esprit, brocade, and all-over beaded lace with nude lining were added to the mix. Necklines became lower and even fell off the shoulder in the now popular look. Splashes of colored beads and bows were added, and designers introduced these elements in their collections.

Lady Diana Spencer's wedding to Price Charles of England in 1981 brought home the possibility of how truly romantic a traditional wedding could be. The entire world was held spellbound when Lady Diana descended from her horse-drawn carriage in her taffeta gown with the seemingly endless twenty- five-foot train, intricately trimmed with thousands of pearls and beads, antique lace, and bows. Lavish, opulent, glittering, luxurious, and bejeweled were the words used to describe her attire. The princess was young and apparently in love, and inspired the romantic in every bride who now longed to be married in a regal and ornate gown and a jeweled veil fit for a queen. No expense seemed too great to achieve that feeling on this most important day. The 1980s was a decade of enormous prosperity and conspicuous consumption, and weddings became more popular than ever.

Considering all this, 1985 was a perfect time for the launch of my collection, St. Pucchi. I set a trend all my own. With my very first collection of all sixteen pieces of colored wedding gowns, I did shock quite a few fashion followers. Without ignoring the bridal tradition, all I did was actually return bridal fashion to its roots, to the times when brides only wore colored gowns to marry in. I chose to mix lavish and fashionable details from past eras, tracing their roots to royalty into my creations. Gowns were full and regal. And my inspiration in those early days was mostly from the Victorian era, since it was the most fashionable, yet traditional. Even though it was a new era, the 1980s bride wished to rekindle a measure of old-world charm and incorporate that look and feel into her special day.

With the 1990s came a change in my own personal life, which was also reflected in my designs. I experimented with many different looks, borrowing details from the past but remaining true to the fashions of the present.

In keeping with my signature look, the designs were elegant and romantic and echoed high fashion, having a look all its own. Bearing in mind diverse personalities, ethnicities and cultures, ages and lifestyles, as well as the venue of the ceremony, there was a dress for every bride.

The St. Pucchi bride was never limited to any one look, as every style was an individual preference, to express her personality and the theme of the occasion. And yet, there was a thread running through each creation, and anyone in the bridal industry looking at a picture of my design instantly recognized it as a St. Pucchi without reading or hearing the name. My gowns continued to evoke timeless old-world elegance with a modern sensibility by blending details from different decades to invoke past-century fantasies for a twentieth-century woman.

I was inspired by pure fantasy and luxurious femininity, whether designing a dramatic ball gown or body-skimming lace sheath. To me, bridal fashion was all about variety, about catering to every whim of the most individual, stylistic instinct of the sophisticated, romantic, or casual bride. There was a style for every bride, giving her an opportunity to express and affirm her identity, to indulge herself by living out her fantasy. The most important goal I wished to achieve was that the bride should feel, and therefore look, beautiful on her most important day—modern, yet classically rooted and personally significant.

When Carolyn Bessette wed John F. Kennedy Jr. in 1996, and walked down the aisle in her pearl-colored silk crêpe floor-length gown, the slim column dress that she wore took the bridal industry by storm. She evoked the image of the bride as a modern icon, and women across the globe wanted to emulate the look as the media and all the magazines featured this as the "new" look in bridal. Even though the look was being worn, it did not see popularity until that day. Brides were somewhat challenged as it was not as forgiving for the full-figured bride; it was more revealing and skimmed the body in such a way that unless you were slim, it would show everything that you felt self-conscious about. Soon, variations of the look came into play, and simple A-line gowns were introduced along with dropped bodice silhouettes.

As more and more women in the new millennium became involved in their careers, the average age when a woman married rose to a worldly twenty-eight, compared to only nineteen in the 1970s, and more women were getting remarried for the second and third time. The bride was a more mature, confident woman, smart and stylish, and she knew exactly what she wanted.

In keeping with the comforts of her personality and style, weddings were not only held in churches and cathedrals, but at beach and mountain resorts, or at their own homes and estates in the presence of their family and friends, often followed by swanky twilight receptions. This gave rise to the need to have different bridal silhouettes that were appropriate and in keeping with the venue and location. No single look was appropriate for all weddings or for every bride.

Through the evolution of fashion, the bridal gown has persistently retained its aura of romance and continued to portray a magical, powerful symbol of love and commitment. Even though some brides opt for a uniquely untraditional gown, they still wish to maintain some aspect of the traditional aesthetic. After all, that dress is ultimately creating a lifetime of memories. Sometimes it becomes an heirloom that is passed from one generation to the next, which is why the traditional is key. A bridal dress must have a timeless feel and maintain its integrity, be well constructed, of good quality material with beautiful details.

Today's modern wedding dresses are much more revealing and open, fueled by a fashion revolution that has ushered in a new era of naked opulence.

Nude has become the new white.

But for how long, I ask?

How long before we become nostalgic and long to look like a real bride again? To embrace tradition and return to deep-rooted values?

After all, fashion is a cycle. And bridal fashion, especially, will always return to its roots.

It's just a matter of time . . .

About the Author

Over thirty years ago, Rani St. Pucchi took the bridal world by storm, despite having no formal training in fashion. She is an award-winning couture fashion designer and founder of the world-renowned bridal house, St. Pucchi. A passionate and dynamic entrepreneur who launched her global empire in the United States in 1985, Rani's vision was to create an avant-garde bridal and evening couture line with modern styling and classic details. That vision has been realized today.

Renowned for infusing her creations with touches of magnificently colored jewels, exquisite hand-embroidery, delicate beading, and sparkling crystals on the finest silks and laces, these inspired designs with innovative draping evoke the timeless elegance every woman desires. As one of the foremost designers to introduce exotic silk fabrics and hand-embroidery, Rani is applauded for being a pioneer in bringing color to the United States bridal scene, having learned that white does not flatter everyone.

Rani has been recognized and nominated on multiple occasions for her design talent and won numerous awards as a Style Innovator. In addition, she has been honored with the Best Bridal Designer Award at the prestigious Chicago Apparel Center's DEBI Awards (Distinctive Excellence in the Bridal Industry).

Rani is famous for designing the wedding dress worn by "Phoebe" as she captured the hearts of millions when she said "I do" in a unique St. Pucchi lilac corset bodice A-line gown on the finale of the hit television show *Friends*.

Her range of avant-garde designs are worn by the world's most discerning celebrity brides and style icons, including Olympic gold medalist Sanya Richards-Ross (wife of New York Giants player Aaron Ross); Candice Crawford (wife of Dallas Cowboys quarterback Tony Romo); actress Tara Reid; Naomi Lowde (wife of Jason Priestley); actress Candice Cameron; and Grammy Award–winning singer-songwriter Alison Krauss, who donned a specially designed Chantilly lace and silk gown at the Country Music Awards.

Rani has enjoyed much media attention. Her signature designs have been recognized in high-profile media outlets such as Entertainment Tonight, *Harper's Bazaar, WWD, Town and Country, Bride's, Cosmopolitan Brides, Inside Weddings, Martha Stewart Weddings,* and *The Knot*.

Having worked with thousands of women, Rani has become well known for her expertise on how a woman's self-image and self-confidence affect her sense of style, her relationships, and her success in life and love. Rani is a relationship expert who is on a mission to empower women and make them feel better about themselves so they can make wise choices.

Rani believes that confidence must start with a woman's love and acceptance of her body and that when a woman is whole and fulfilled in herself, she makes better relationship choices.

Writing has always been Rani St. Pucchi's passion. Since she majored in English literature and poetry, it was inevitable that she would add the role of a number-one bestselling author to her roster of accomplishments.

In addition to the book you are reading now, Rani is the author of *Your Body, Your Style: Simple Tips on Dressing to Flatter Your*

Body Type. Renowned for her savvy knowledge of a woman's form and fit, Rani shares her knowledge of more than three decades with all women so they can make better styling choices.

In her second book, *The SoulMate Checklist: Keys to Finding Your Perfect Partner*, Rani walks women through their journey to finding true soul mate love. She holds her readers by the hand, guiding them step by step on every phase of the path they must navigate before reaching that place of bliss.

Her upcoming books include:

- ***Secrets About Success Every Woman Should Know***
- ***Unveiled: A Celebrity Fashion Designer's Story: A Memoir of My Life's Journey***

Born and raised in Bangkok, Thailand, Rani now happily lives in Los Angeles, California.

Learn more about Rani at www.ranistpucchi.com.

Also by Rani St. Pucchi

Your Body, Your Style:
Simple Tips on Dressing to Flatter Your Body Type

RANI ST. PUCCHI teaches you simple tricks on how to dress your body in a way that will enhance your best assets and camouflage areas that you feel uncomfortable about or find lacking in any way.

Elevate your self-confidence by defining your personal style and becoming clear on how you wish to be seen in the world.

Learn a simple process to determine what colors flatter you most and which ones to part with so that you may look more interesting, more assured, and in control.

Receive smart shopping tips, learn the importance of investing in the right lingerie, immerse yourself in simple style advice for your body type and more …

Embrace your unique personality and shine with your body and your style.

The Soulmate Checklist:
Keys to Finding Your Perfect Partner

RANI ST. PUCCHI delves into the meaning of Soul Mate relationships as she guides you on a quest for love that lasts a lifetime.

Are images of the ideal relationship just fantasy, or do they have a basis in truth?

Does everyone have a perfect Soul Mate who is waiting to be found by him or her, or is a "perfect" relationship something that one must develop with oneself first?

Getting beyond the "in love" phase—will the relationship last?

Questions like these and many others are addressed here as Rani provides insights into the nature of personal relationships and Soul Mate love.

The *SoulMate Checklist* will help you avoid misconceptions about love, find the blueprint for coming to terms with your past, experience unconditional love, and find out what a Soul Mate is—and isn't.

www.ingramcontent.com/pod-product-compliance
Lightning Source LLC
Chambersburg PA
CBHW042227010526
44113CB00044B/2739